JEWELLERY moves

ornament for the 21st century

AMANDA GAME AND ELIZABETH GORING

NMS Publishing

Published by NMS Publishing Limited,
National Museums of Scotland,
Chambers Street, Edinburgh EH1 1JF

British Library Cataloguing in Publication Data
A catalogue record of this book is available
from the British Library

ISBN 1 901663 03 5

Designed by Artisan Graphics, Edinburgh

Printed by Craft Print Pte Ltd, Singapore

CONTENTS

INTRODUCTION

Jewellery Moves is about ways of looking at and enjoying contemporary studio jewellery. The authors, one from a national museum, the other from a private gallery, share a personal passion for studio jewellery and the achievements of its creators, inspired by thirty years' combined experience. The selection includes work made between 1993-98 by about 130 jewellers, practising in 24 different countries. Such a selection is necessarily personal but offers insight into a rich, varied, and little documented area of the arts.

What is jewellery?

Jewellery is the collective noun for a series of relatively small scale objects which can be attached to clothing, or worn directly on the body, for personal adornment. Jewellery is both a concept — adornment — and an object — the jewel.

The art of jewellery is probably the most ancient human art of all and is practised all over the world.

Long before people made and decorated pottery, or created and decorated cloth, they used natural objects such as shells, stones or flowers to decorate themselves, recognizing how such ornaments could transform the wearer and invest him or her with power and, often, magical status.

Today the jeweller's art is still practised all over the world. Jewellery's importance to humans throughout their history is illustrated by the burial of jewellery in graves, the named bequests of jewellery in wills and the tendency of jewels to be preserved by successive generations, even if the original value and meaning have been lost.

What is studio jewellery?

For the purposes of this book, the term 'studio jewellery' means jewellery produced by individuals, working in their own studios, usually alone, at most with one or two assistants, who deliberately control every aspect of producing a piece of jewellery from original idea to finished work.

The rise of the studio jewellery movement has been particularly marked from the 1960s onwards and reflects both the changes in art education — studio jewellers are likely to have received an art college training rather than a traditional commercial apprenticeship - and wider social changes in fashion and lifestyle which have created demands for different work.

Studio jewellery is characterised by a concern for individuality. The individual maker produces the individual objects to be worn by individuals. The work may be made in a wide range of materials, in many forms, and may communicate a vast array of different ideas, but the valuing of the individual is an underlying concern of studio jewellery and thus all the works in *Jewellery Moves*.

Where is it from?

Although studio jewellery has been selected from twenty-four countries, vast areas of the world are not represented, including Africa, much of Asia, the Indian sub-continent, most of the Middle East, South America and parts of Eastern Europe. Why?

There are significant social, cultural, political and economic factors which preclude the production of studio jewellery, as defined here, in these areas: a lack of demand for specialised individual work, the absence of appropriate training, and particular perceptions of the place of the individual. Superb jewellery, for example, is produced in India, which has a distinguished tradition of the highest quality work. Skilful and beautiful as much of it is, however, it rarely bears the name of the individual maker, and jewellers have the correspondingly low status of the anonymous artisan.

Studio jewellery appears where there is a tradition of valuing the work of the named individual artist. In Western Europe, the relatively high social status of painters and sculptors can be traced back to the Renaissance. In the Middle Ages and earlier, painters and sculptors, together with woodcarvers, potters and jewellers, were largely anonymous artisans. During the Renaissance painters and sculptors rose to join the social ranks of poets, rhetoricians and philosophers. With occasional notable exceptions, it was not until the Arts & Crafts Movement of the nineteenth century and more particularly the Studio Crafts Movement of the twentieth century that the named individual potter, glassmaker and jeweller began to achieve comparable social status. In Oriental cultures the talented individual artist has always been appreciated, and in Japan master craftspeople, like other great artists, may be awarded the highest artistic accolade of National Living Treasure.

Geographical boundaries are, however, beginning to blur in studio jewellery. Many of the pieces in this book demonstrate that studio jewellers draw on a multiplicity of cultural influences in their work. Sometimes this results from an exploration of an artist's own ethnic roots. But many radical experiments in jewellery, as in all the arts, rest on the foundations of different cultures. Two books on the jewellery and adornment of India and Africa are included in the further reading list specifically to throw light on some of these influences.

Why here and now?

Jewellery has a distinctive and ancient history in Scotland, both in the materials used and in certain styles of work such as 'plaid brooches' and 'luckenbooth' brooches. Leading members of the studio jewellery movement have been working in Scotland since the 1960s and notable training grounds for studio jewellers exist in Scotland's four main art schools in Aberdeen, Dundee, Edinburgh and Glasgow.

As we move towards the end of the twentieth century, with a devolved Scottish parliament in prospect, interest is growing in all forms of art practised in Scotland. It seems an appropriate moment to assess the achievements of Scottish studio jewellers in an international context.

Structure and thesis of Jewellery Moves

An interest in identifying the preoccupations which lie behind the creation and wearing of studio jewellery today has encouraged the authors to abandon the more traditional arrangement of work by artist, country, material or technique. Instead the book is arranged by themes, intended to offer useful insights and suggest ideas.

The framework of *Material, Form, Idea & Image* and *The Body* is a useful way of organising a vast range of sometimes quite disparate material into a manageable structure. The themes are not comprehensive: every commentator would have their own suggestions for further ones. Nor does any single piece of jewellery fit conveniently or solely under one theme. The placing of particular works within specific themes represents just one way of approaching them. In each case there has been an assessment of what seems to be the dominant theme in a given piece of work, and to categorise accordingly.

Jewellery, unlike other art forms, is placed directly on the human body. Although the scale and content of the objects illustrated in *Jewellery Moves* varies greatly, all are united by the fact that they are designed to be worn. Static, and put out of reach behind glass in a case, jewellery loses much of its power. It is meant to hang from an ear, rest against skin, encircle a wrist, move and turn, be run through the fingers. Detailed photographs may emphasise

technical skill, display cases may emphasise the beauty of its form, but jewellery can only reach its full potential when it is handled, moved and worn. The specially commissioned portrait photographs by Carol Gordon are intended to highlight this essential nature of jewellery.

A short section of the book is devoted to technique and process. Under technique, some of the different skills practised by studio jewellers are examined. (A more general glossary of technical terms is also provided.) Process, the journey from original idea to finished object, is discussed with reference to some of the various jewellers included in

the book. The discussion of process also emphasises that there is rarely a 'right' way of doing things. Give ten people a work bench, some basic training and tools, and you will arrive at ten very different works.

Studio jewellery, like all fine and applied arts, exists within a marketplace. The penultimate section of this book examines questions of access and context for studio jewellery. Who promotes or buys work? How does this affect what is available? Most importantly, who might wear the work? This is not an aspect generally considered in the history of jewellery, yet it is crucially important to what we are able to see, to enjoy and to value.

MATERIAL

Jane, Choreographer *Necklace, Brigitte Turba*

Jewellery, unlike ceramics or glass, is not materially defined. Yet probably the first question that many of us ask about a piece of jewellery is what is it made of? A large proportion of jewellery is judged and prized on material value. Assessing the materials illustrated in *Jewellery Moves* allows us to consider this idea. If we do place greater value, in every sense of that word, on certain materials, why do we do this? No material is, after all, intrinsically valuable. When we talk of certain materials being traditional to the jeweller's art, to which tradition are we referring? We can all think of wonderful jewellery which is made from bone and ceramic as well as stone and gold.

There are few materials modern studio jewellers do not consider possible for their work. A lot of the materials occur naturally, but there is also extensive use of synthetics — in fact the development of synthetic materials can be said to have had a significant impact on jewellery design from early Bakelite to modern Colorcore. All the materials, however, whether expensive (gold, certain stones) or cheap (discarded telephone directories, driftwood) are valued sufficiently by different jewellers for them to lavish hours of thought and workmanship on them to create pieces. Material value, as much as beauty, is in the eye of the beholder.

ALCHEMY

*By happy of alchemy
of mind
They turn to pleasure all they
find*

MATTHEW GREEN

Early alchemists were driven by the desire to transform and alter material properties — most notably the search for the philosopher's stone. The word 'alchemy' suggests a magical transformation and seems an appropriate word to use to describe some studio jewellery. In this section we celebrate the jewellery artists who take a material which is essentially worthless, in commercial terms, and transform it into something of value through their artistry.

Paper is a medium universally used by artists whether as a surface for a graphic image or as a material in itself to be cut, coloured, scored and folded. Its very familiarity can make us ignore its potential. Paper is central to the work of Dutch artist Nel Linssen and Finnish artist Janna Syvänoja. Linssen cuts and folds coloured paper into repeating elements which are pierced and folded on to

elasticised wire, which remains invisible, but provides the necessary flexible element for the wearer. The stack of paper bangles (1) extends our vision of paper as a material capable of producing sophisticated and elegant jewellery.

1 **Nel Linssen**
Stack of 10 Bangles 1996
Paper, silicon tube, 80×25mm

2 **Janna Syvänoja**
Jewellery 1995–1997
Paper, steel, 150mm

3 **Gilles Jonemann**
Rings 1997
Quail's egg, silver, 26×35mm

Janna Syvänoja works with used paper, such as discarded telephone directories, to create work which shares the rhythmic quality of Linssen's work, though it relies on tone, rather than colour, for effect. As with Linssen's work, it is the care with which the work is constructed, the consideration of shapes, and the combination of shapes into three-dimensional forms, which create the magic (2). Syvänoja also uses naturally occurring materials such as seeds and bark, and her ability to create new images with these materials extends our appreciation of jewellery as well as of the materials themselves.

French artist Gilles Jonemann's attitude to material is eclectic. An earlier body of work made extensive use of papier mâché, but he randomly selects stones, eggs, metal — anything which allows him to express his particular vision of jewellery. At all times he tries to create a sense of value through being alert to the possibilities of different materials. Often in his work there is a tension between opposite values — synthetic/natural, chaos/harmony, modern/traditional — and he selects and combines materials which express this tension (3). The fragile eggs are placed where one would expect to find hard stones in some traditional European jewellery. In this new setting, the egg becomes transformed into a lasting as well as precious object.

Like Jonemann, the German jeweller Dorothea Pruehl selects a wide range of materials and explores their expressive qualities. The piece shown (4) is made from titanium — a hard metal developed industrially as the outer casing for aircraft. Pruehl has cut a series of randomly shaped elements which are then coloured to a dull but lustrous grey and assembled to create the final form. The physical hardness of this industrial material appears transformed, by the artist's hand, into a sensuous and expressive jewellery material.

4 **Dorothea Pruehl**
Titanium Chain III 1997
Titanium, ivory, 750mm

The Swiss artist Verena Sieber-Fuchs and the German-born but Irish-based artist Brigitte Turba both use discarded or waste materials as a source for their work. The transformation of discards into decorative objects is not, in itself, new. There is a widespread domestic craft tradition of such transformation, shown in objects such as rag rugs and quilts. It is less common, in Western society at least, with jewellery. For Sieber-Fuchs, old pill packaging, sweet wrappers or photographic film (5) create rich possibilities of colour and texture, and she weaves these unlikely materials into bold and exotic jewellery. She and Turba, who uses cut-up and shaped plastic water bottles (6) both use recycled materials as a comment on the waste of society as well as for their material possibilities.

Scottish-born, Canadian-based, jeweller Alison Bailey Smith constructs elaborate and ceremonial jewellery from industrial wire. Her materials are often gathered from sources such as abandoned television sets and she succeeds, like Turba and Sieber-Fuchs, in creating beauty out of waste.

5 **Verena Sieber-Fuchs**
Am Rande des Films
Collar 1997
Film, Wire, 360mm dia.

6 **Brigitte Turba**
Bracelet 1996
Plastic bottles, nylon wire,
130×130×25mm

CHARACTER

*Passion could bring
character enough*

WILLIAM BUTLER YEATS

For some jewellers certain materials provide a lifelong subject of study. Quintessential properties such as colour, malleability, structural hardness, flexibility have drawn these artists to a material. Works made in this spirit can contribute to both technical development and also to the development of a new aesthetic appreciation of the character of the material.

Metal is an enduring material for jewellery. Precious metals, such as silver and gold, have been widely used by jewellers from antiquity to the present day. Their widespread use is due, at least in part, to their essential physical properties. Studio jewellers who study these essential properties in depth, through the eye of the artist and the hand of the maker, enhance our appreciation of silver and gold as expressive materials for contemporary jewellery.

Two such jewellers are Toril Bjorg from Norway and Jacqueline Mina from England. It may be unsurprising that Bjorg, as a Scandinavian, should choose silver as her jewellery material. Yet her ability to work with both silver sheet and wire in imaginative ways distinguishes her jewellery from much modern commercial work. Bjorg uses a traditional Norwegian technique of knotless knitting with silver wire to build up flexible structures which are often contrasted with elements constructed from silver sheet. The resulting work (7) has a power and presence not often achieved in silver jewellery.

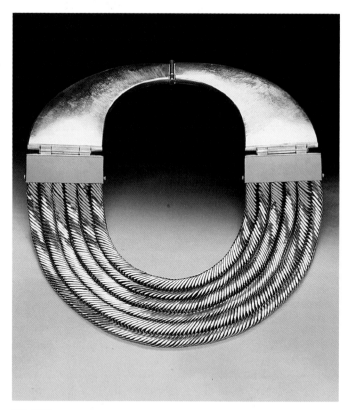

7 **Toril Bjorg**
Necklace 1996
Silver, 240×300mm

Jacqueline Mina has devoted over twenty-five years to exploring gold, perhaps the most universal of all jewellery materials. Through her pioneering use of different techniques, such as fusion inlay with platinum and gold (8), she has both added to technical research and extended the visual possibilities of her material. She is a good example of what the craft and design critic David Pye was describing when he spoke of the craftsman as 'laboratory for new ideas'. By her confident handling of the material Mina creates jewellery which is expressive, sensual and beautifully crafted.

Japan has a distinguished tradition of metalcraft, which is internationally admired and recognised. Many techniques involving the colouring and bonding of different metals, now widely used in Western studio jewellery, are Japanese in origin. Despite the significance of metalwork in Japanese culture, however, there has been no parallel tradition of jewellery making. It is only in recent years that jewellery has gained importance as an independent branch of artistic activity and Japanese jewellery artists have begun to interpret their traditional crafts such as lacquerwork, metalwork and

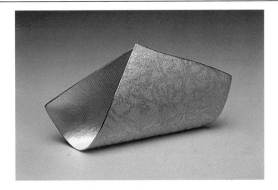

8 **Jacqueline Mina**
Brooch 1998
18ct gold, platinum, 64×32mm

papermaking through the forms of modern studio jewellery. An important artist in making these links has been Yasuki Hiramatsu. His knowledge of traditional metalcraft allows him to push and play against the boundaries of what the material can physically do and in the process create extraordinary new jewellery. He hammers silver and gold sheet until very thin and manipulates it into collars, cuffs (9) and brooches, which seem to hover and shimmer against the body like gossamer threads.

9 **Yasuki Hiramatsu**
Bangle 1991
Silver, resin, 100×43mm
NMS Collection

Robert Smit works in Amsterdam, a city which, unlike Japan, has historic connections with the jewellery trade. Paradoxically, Amsterdam is home to both the most conventional commercial jewellery trade (as a centre for the diamond industry) and also to some of the most radical movements in studio jewellery, aided by the pioneering efforts of individuals such as Paul Derrez at Galerie Ra. Smit seems to balance these two elements, by working with a highly traditional jewellery material, gold, but working with it in a way that is anything but traditional. Although the use of conventional jewellery materials such as gold was rejected by New Jewellers in the 1970s, Smit continued to be drawn to the character of gold, and after a period of twelve years away from jewellery in the 1980s, has returned with renewed vigour to the field. His work exudes the disrespectful confidence of the true artist. He scores, folds, paints, varnishes and abrades gold sheet in ways that few have the courage, or ability, to do: the very history, and commercial value, of gold often inhibits such a free, imaginative approach. Smit's images are witty, figurative and intimate (10) and his work

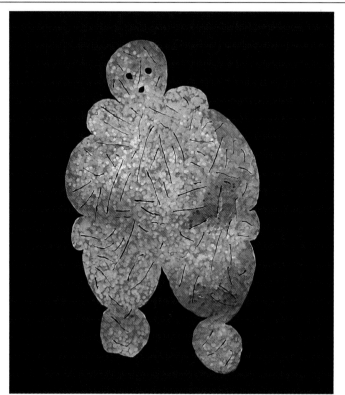

10 **Robert Smit**
Fat Man Brooch 1997
Gold, 135×80×5mm

11 **Pavel Opočenský**
Brooch 1996
Chalcedony, 100×20×20mm

imaginatively binds tradition and innovation.

Pavel Opočenský was born, and now works, in the Czech Republic but spent many years living and working in America. He works both as a sculptor and a jeweller carving a variety of natural materials (and occasionally synthetics such as Colorcore) to create resonant simple forms and his work has been described as showing 'the extreme simplification of constructivism'. Although, as a Czech, the influence of this formal style would not be surprising, it is his exploration of the character of different stones, through the process of carving, that seems to dominate. Using diamond saw drills, Opočenský cuts into the stone, in ways which accentuate the natural form and rhythm of the material, like a sculptor carving into a block of marble. The subtly layered structures created, work as striking pieces of jewellery (11) by the addition of simple metal pins or fastenings.

Australian Catherine Truman spent a period working with a traditional netsuke carver in Japan. This has given her the confidence to carve and shape wood on a small scale, and to understand the process of carving in harmony with the rhythm of a natural material. Her limewood brooches (12) celebrate the tactility of the material and the energy of the process of carving. It is not of course only natural materials that can be shaped by carving, Opočenský has used Colorcore and his fellow Czech artist, René Hora, carves cellulose acetate — a material more commonly moulded in jewellery (13). In Hora's case the formal flexibility of the synthetic is an attraction, and he enjoys the tension of exploring different man-made forms in the scale and materials of modern jewellery.

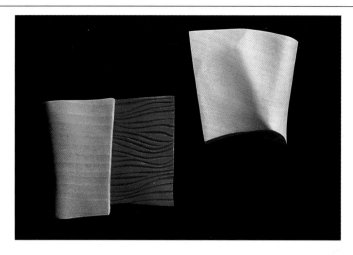

12 **Catherine Truman**
Brooches 1996
English limewood, *shu niku* ink
40×40×5mm

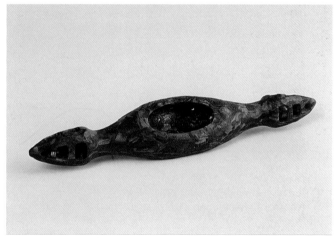

13 **René Hora**
Kayak Brooch 1997
Cellulose acetate 160×30×15mm

14 Joyce Chateauvert
Eve Necklace (detail)
Abaca paper, silver 110mm

15 Beppe Kessler
Brooches 1996
Textile, wood, acrylic, graphite, gold
leaf, stone 40×40mm

American Joyce Chateauvert, and Dutch artist Beppe Kessler have both devoted many years to studying materials less commonly associated with jewellery. Chateauvert explores a particular type of paper, made from the abaca plant. Abaca paper is mostly used for making tea bags and cables, as the plant has fibres that are naturally resistant to water.

This physical quality attracted Chateauvert. Additionally, paper made from the fibre has both translucence and lightness (14) which makes it an effective material for jewellery.

Kessler studied textiles at the Rietveld Academy in Amsterdam and she continues to design for the textile industry in the Netherlands. For her, jewellery is another way of exploring fabric in relation to the body. In recent works (15) Kessler wraps stones and other objects in different fabrics, and then paints, stretches and cuts the fabric to reveal the hidden objects. By this method, she creates tactile, mysterious pieces which retain the visual fluidity of draped cloth, while having striking formal presence.

Joan Parcher, another American, is fascinated by the essential character of different materials, and how these can be worked to produce unusual contemporary jewellery. A recent body of work has made use of mica, a naturally occurring silicate mineral. By working with the plate-like layered structure of the mineral, she creates shimmering, translucent necklaces (16) which are light to wear and extremely tactile.

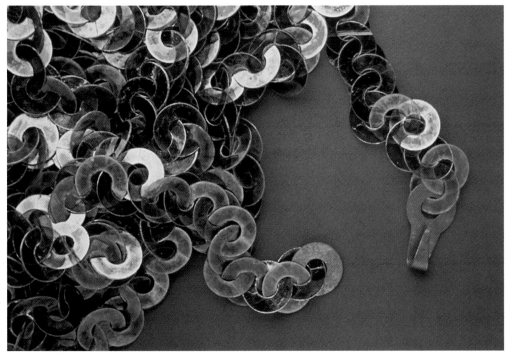

16 **Joan Parcher**
Chain 1996
18ct gold, mica, 21×2743mm

Peter Hoogeboom, from the Netherlands, constructs collars and cuffs from moulded ceramic elements. He was drawn to clay by its formal flexibility — it can, when raw, be moulded to many shapes — and by its fragility. Clay objects, even when fired to high temperatures, need to be handled with care. For Hoogeboom, the fragility of the fired clay acts as a metaphor for the transience of life (17).

17 **Peter Hoogeboom**
Mother Dao Necklace 1995
Ceramic, silver, brass, iron, 520×50×250mm

COLOUR

The purest and most thoughtful minds are those that love colour

John Ruskin

Many different materials are used by jewellers to introduce colour to their work. In traditional jewellery, stones are valued according to the particular richness of colour — the deep red of rubies, the grass green of emeralds, the rich blue of lapis lazuli, for example. Paint and dye can be directly applied to a range of surfaces including metal, fabric and paper. For metalsmiths, there is the traditional technique of enamelling, in which ground-up glass powder is applied like a skin to the surface of the metal. The metals themselves can be selected for colour: yellow and red gold alloys, the greys of steel, platinum and silver. Metals can be coloured by chemicals (patinated), or altered by abrasion, to achieve tone and contrast. The most vivid and varied colours can be achieved through use of the vast array of synthetics: acrylic, Colorcore, nylon, perspex.

Australian jeweller Robert Baines applies dry pigment as a powder coat to silver wire to achieve his vibrant red brooches (18). Red is a colour associated with energy, masculinity, danger: it is a colour that leaps out of the spectrum and makes objects appear nearer than they are. A brilliant red brooch will attract attention and encourage the viewer to look at the piece more closely: in this case to enjoy the intricate structure and patterning made with the silver wire.

French artist Monika Brugger chooses to work with

18 **Robert Baines**
Redline No 29
Brooch 1997 Silver, pigment, 190×150mm

21

silver because of its colour. The image of silver as a jewellery material suggesting a certain mood of modern understatement can be traced to the influence of post-war Scandinavian work. Silver is, after all, seen in a rather different way if associated with ornate silver tableware. However, Brugger, like many contemporary jewellers, sees the colour of silver as pure and impartial; when handled in a certain way it can create feelings of contemplation and reflection. Her chemically whitened and pierced brooches (19) play on this association.

Italian artist Annamaria Zanella creates jewellery which encapsulates the energy of colour in bold, gestural brushstrokes. She combines strips of rusted steel or coloured silver with strips of brilliantly pigmented gold. The contrast of texture, colour and tone in her work (20) gives the work its immense vitality and power.

Both the American James Bennett and the Scottish artist Mark Powell explore colour through the use of the traditional technique of enamelling on gold and silver. The skill and patience demanded by this intricate technique tend to mitigate against very expressive jewellery. However, in the right hands, as Bennett's Jurjani Brooch (21) illustrates, enamel can be used to create works that are both fluid and painterly.

21 **James Bennett**
Jurjani Brooch 1996
Enamel, gold, 38×70mm

19 **Monika Brugger**
Silence 6
Brooch 1997 Silver, 90mm

20 **Annamaria Zanella**
Brooch 1997
Silver, niello, enamel,
pigment, gold, 65×68×15mm

Shinya Yamamura from Japan uses another traditional technique to provide brilliant colour, but in his case it is lacquer, not enamel. Lacquer was traditionally used in Japan to make small decorative objects. Yamamura uses it to create striking modern jewellery (22) by forming simple shapes from wood and building up depth of colour with the pigmented lacquer. The final surface of each piece is often worked with *makie* and *raden* to achieve the desired brilliance.

Peter Chang from Glasgow and American Marjorie Schick explore colour exclusively through non-precious materials. Schick builds up layers of papier mâché over a styrofoam or card shape to create dramatic forms which are then painted in vibrant colours. Her ability to handle both bold colour and form creates jewellery of considerable expressive power (23). Chang uses plastics. Recycled toys and other plastic ephemera are reconstructed into bold, brilliant pieces of jewellery. He is attracted to plastic because of its virtuosity as a material. It can become anything, be any colour. His training as a sculptor enables him to create new forms with ferocious confidence. The

22 **Shinya Yamamura**
No 4 Red Brooch 1996
Lacquer, cypress wood, gold
85×40×24mm

23 **Marjorie Schick**
Edged Wave Armlet 1995
Papier mâché, 257×190×125mm

bangle (24) is a jewel of our times. Eclectic, witty, brilliant, slightly disturbing: it seems to attract our attention like the mating display of some exotic insect.

English jeweller Dawn Gulyas is also attracted by the versatility of plastics. In her case, brilliantly coloured, organic forms are created by covering balsawood with several layers of pigmented polyester resin. Like lacquer, the layers are applied then sanded back several times to achieve the final colours and texture. Bold colours are influenced by the brilliance of tropical fish and flowers (25).

Another English jeweller, Jane Adam, draws her inspiration for vibrant colour and pattern from the traditional textiles of India. She selects aluminium, a metal in itself grey-toned, and builds up a brilliant spectrum of colour through using inks, dyes and anodising processes. Her most recent work (26) explores texture as well as colour through the controlled melting of the surface of the aluminium.

25 **Dawn Gulyas**
Brooch 1994
Balsa wood, polyester resin, 90×115×40mm

24 **Peter Chang**
Bangle 1996
PVC, perspex, resin, silver, 160mm

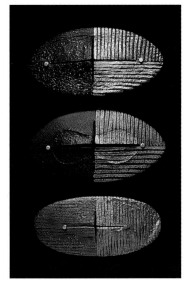

26 **Jane Adam**
3 brooches 1997
Aluminium, largest 90×40mm

CULTURAL VALUE

*Art is not only made
one way, art is a
point of view*

MARIANNE WEREFKIN

In studio jewellery the question of the cultural value of different materials, how they are valued by society, has been an important influence. The New Jewellery Movement in the 1970s was concerned with ways of challenging our preconceptions about cultural value. At the end of the twentieth century, perceptions about cultural value of the arts in general are constantly in flux, which influences all artists including studio jewellers.

In this section, we consider how some jewellers may value certain materials traditional to their culture, whilst others range freely through the world of materials to select whatever best suits their particular intention. It is worth remembering that whatever the makers' views of the cultural value of the material, the onlookers' views may be different. For example, for many people gold has an inescapable resonance of tradition, plastic an equally inescapable resonance of disposability.

Robert Baines has devoted over twenty-five years of research to the ancient technique of gold granulation, practised by early peoples such as the Etruscans. His fascination with this particular use of gold, and how it has been valued by different cultures throughout history, has created an important body of research. He has recently completed a Fulbright scholarship at the Metropolitan Museum in New York analysing granulated work in the collection. As both a historian and a maker, Baines provides a useful bridge to the understanding of jewellery in different cultures.

Gijs Bakker, the Dutch jeweller, is inspired by twentieth-century European culture. At the forefront of experimental jewellery in the 1960s and 1970s, Bakker's aluminium and plastic space age collars and cuffs were icons for the time just like a Paco Rabanne dress or the model Twiggy. He celebrated the modernity of the materials and the modern technology often used to create them. He continues to explore a contemporary idiom for jewellery by using computer modelling techniques (CAD/CAM) to create new forms and ways of forming (27).

27 Gijs Bakker
Shot 2
Bangle 1997 Nylon, 83mm

28 **Liv Blåvarp**
Neckpiece 1997
Dyed maple, 250mm

29 **Rowena Gough**
Channel Tryst-Rope 1997
Silver, mother-of-pearl shell buttons,
1500×35×10mm

Liv Blåvarp uses wood: a material which allows certain expressive possibilities and is also important to her as a Norwegian. There is a long-standing tradition of using timber for both buildings and decorative carved objects in Norway. Blåvarp carves and dyes maple or birch into small-scale elements which are threaded on to silk or wire to produce flexible collars which explore the beauty of the material (28).

Australian jeweller Rowena Gough constructs sensual neckpieces from mother-of-pearl shell buttons. Pearl shell buttons were once an indispensable part of clothing in the West — fastening clothing from boots to evening gowns. In the late nineteenth and early twentieth century, Australia supplied over seventy-five per cent of the world's shell buttons: a vast trade which seriously depleted Pacific shell stocks. By reusing these now discarded buttons, Gough considers questions of material value and cultural appropriation (29).

German artist Katja Korsawe is interested in materials which have been traditional to jewellery, such as human hair (as in the eighteenth and nineteenth-century use of woven hair in mourning jewellery) and parts of animals, but are no longer in widespread use in many cultures through a change in notions of acceptability. Her extraordinary and flexible necklaces (30) made from pigs bladder and hair are beautiful, and disturbing when one realises their material content.

30 **Katja Korsawe**
Necklace 1997
Tanned pig's bladder, 100mm

The increased possibility of travel for artists today has increased the crosscultural influences in much contemporary art. The Danish artist Anette Kraen is an inveterate traveller. Her work exemplifies this with a structural formality indicative of Danish work, but the materials she uses, such as lacquer, horsehair (31), silk and bone, are drawn from her experiences of other cultures. Recent pieces combine Japanese lacquer with horsehair.

Kiwon Wang is a Korean American jeweller. She makes jewellery from combining waste materials, such as old newspapers, with traditional materials such as silver and gold. She sees the combination of the two potentially incompatible materials into a resolved whole as a metaphor for the synthesis of her Eastern and Western cultural ancestors — and by extension a synthesis of those cultures themselves (32).

31 **Anette Kraen**
Necklace 1995
Pigmented horsehair, silver, gold leaf, 190×30mm

32 **Kiwon Wang**
Pin 1997
Silver, rice-paper, ink, 76×76×51mm

FORM

Phil, Artist *Brooch, Dorothy Hogg*

Art is nothing without Form

Gustave Flaubert

Form is both the shape of an object and the space it occupies. Formal language is to the visual artist what words are to the writer: it is the way that meaning and excitement are created — much as it is with the choice of material, or the use of colour. Form is determined by many things, such as material and technology, as well as the intention of the artist. Twentieth-century art has been a history of movements, involved in defining an appropriate formal language for the time. Modernism, Constructivism, Cubism — movements which include art, architecture, design and the decorative arts — all address themselves to the vocabulary of form. Jewellers, as much as painters, potters or sculptors, have absorbed these debates and allowed them to stimulate new ideas for work.

Importantly, jewellery forms are dictated by the body. The most elaborate African ornament or opulent European jewel are both formed around the idea of a human body. That said, the range of scale, shapes, materials and ideas contained by the forms is vast. Sometimes jewellery is designed to reform the body by stretching its contours as in the neck rings of some African tribal jewellery: sometimes jewellery is made an indelible part of the body, as with tattooing. But the body remains the defining space for jewellery.

BALANCE

*What I dream of is
an art of balance*

HENRI MATISSE

Jewellery will be worn on a moving body, and how it balances as the body moves can be an essential quality of the work. In addition jewellery, in common with all the arts, achieves visual balance by the successful composition of different elements.

Scottish jeweller Dorothy Hogg and English jeweller Maria Hanson, though separated by a generation, share a common approach to formal balance, influenced by European modernism. Both women work with silver, creating work which is a delight to wear, yet retains a formal seriousness, aptly described by Hogg as an 'austere sensuality'. Hogg's Spirit Level brooches (33) are an encapsulation of this. The different silver elements are free-hanging within the elliptical structure and move and shift with the movement of the body. Hanson's rings (34) are held into the hand by a broad silver bar rather than by a conventional circular shank which will influence the movement and gestures of the wearer. Hanson's silver elements are more voluptuous, more rounded than Hogg's Spirit Level brooch, yet retain a similar formality, both while static and in movement.

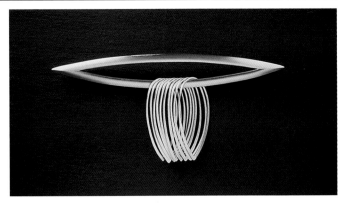

33 **Dorothy Hogg**
Spirit Level Brooch 1994
Silver, 100×45 mm

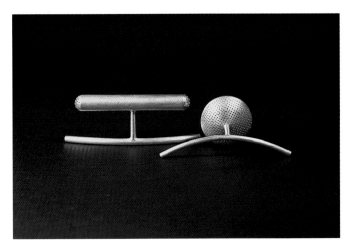

34 **Maria Hanson**
Reversal 1 & 2
Rings 1995
Silver, 30×30×20mm/60×15×15mm

Another English jeweller, Elizabeth Callinicos, explores balance with a series of neckpieces in silver and fibre (35). The two hollow contrasting silver elements balance each side of the body — front and back — like weights and thus give visual interest in the round. The necklace moves softly with the body, but the weight of the different forms keeps the piece well balanced.

Balance is a motivation behind the work of Korean jeweller, Jung-Gyu Yi. Her silver brooches (36) explore the tension between light and shade, angle and curve, space and mass. The balance between these different elements, evident in the static object, shifts and changes as the light falls on the moving body and sets up new formal relationships.

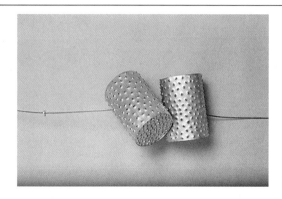

35 **Elizabeth Callinicos**
2 Cylinder Neckpiece 1997
Silver, 55×13mm

36 **Jung-Gyu Yi**
A Memory of Fall No 4
Brooch 1996
Silver, 24ct gold foil, 100×107×18mm

HARMONY

*Such harmony is in
immortal souls*

WILLIAM SHAKESPEARE

Some works of art, particularly formally abstract works, seem to defy the written word. Quite often there is consensus about the profound experience of abstract art, but there is rarely consensual language within which to discuss it. Harmony suggests both beauty and a sense of resolution, revealing mastery of the essentially visual language of abstract art.

Italian artist Francesco Pavan uses coloured gold alloys to create striking brooches (37). Gold sheet is cut into strips and woven into repeating geometric patterns, with the surface of the gold abraded to enhance tonal values. Basic forms and patterns are inextricably linked to create a chromatic progression which shifts and changes with the movement of the body. Pavan's work is a beautiful and powerful distillation of the techniques and ideas essential to the goldsmith's art.

Catherine Martin, the English artist, trained as a musician and then as a *kumihimo* artist in Japan, working with the traditional silk threads. She began experimenting with braiding gold and platinum wire in the early 1990s and her ability to adapt *kumihimo* techniques to metal wire, has resulted in jewellery of considerable interest. She works directly with the wire, often braiding for ten to twelve-hour stretches, using the rhythm of music to aid her concentration. The long braids are then

37 **Francesco Pavan**
Intersecting Laminae Brooch 1992
Gold, 112×102×13mm

38 Catherine Martin
Necklace 1995
18ct gold, 172mm
NMS Collection

manipulated into the final piece with the work reflecting something of the meditative rhythm involved in making it (38).

English jeweller Wendy Ramshaw is internationally renowned for her imaginative modern rings. For over thirty years, she has refined and developed this form of jewellery, finding new and powerful combinations of shape, colour, texture and tone. All the different rings contained within the sets are separate and can be moved around to create new combinations when worn on the finger. The work, when not worn, sits on beautifully designed turned perspex or metal stands, which give it a marked presence off as well as on the body (39).

39 **Wendy Ramshaw**
Destination
Set of 3 Ringsets 1997
Sychroniser 18ct gold, cubic zirconium, perspex
Moment 18ct gold, perspex
Indicator 18ct gold, cubic zirconium, tantalum, niobium
160mm×65mm

German goldsmith Herman Jünger views metal as an infinitely flexible and supple substance, which demands a similarly flexible artistic approach. The pendant (40) typifies his ability to create resonant work out of the simplest of forms and shapes: an ability underpinned by knowledge, skill and a constant receptiveness to new ideas. He talks of the infinite reservoir of pattern, rhythm and forms which exists in the world around us, which provides constant inspiration to him, the artist, and through him, to us.

Austrian-born, English artist Gerda Flöckinger, uses her immense technical confidence as a goldsmith to create vital and original jewellery. She has developed her own techniques involving the controlled fusion of gold and silver to achieve the rich surface textures characteristic of her work. With her unique artist's eye for composition, she combines these with precious and semi-precious stones to produce work (41) which is simultaneously voluptuous and formally satisfying.

40 **Herman Jünger**
Pendant 1996
Gold, palladium, 150×120×40mm

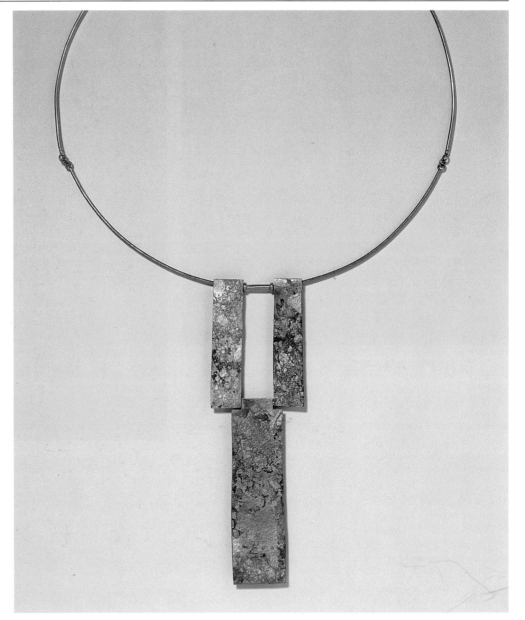

English jeweller David Watkins has been an important influence on British jewellery, through his work at the Royal College of Art in London, and also, like Flöckinger, through his intellectually rigorous approach to making. Closely involved with the New Jewellery Movement of the 1970s, he experimented with modern materials such as Neoprene and Colorcore to develop a new formal language for jewellery. He has also made longstanding use of the computer as a design tool, combining this with hand techniques to create beautifully resonant work (42).

41 **Gerda Flöckinger**
Ring 1993
18ct gold, moonstone, diamonds, 23×20mm
Ring 1993
18ct gold, diamonds, cultured pearl, 12×20mm

42 **David Watkins**
Wheel Pin 1998
Gold, 110mm

LINE

*An active line on a walk
moving freely*

PAUL KLEE

English jeweller Cynthia Cousens hammers and forges lengths of silver wire to different thicknesses to create necklaces. Two years ago Cousens began to experiment with evoking the quality of the drawn line in her jewellery, after an intensive period spent studying and drawing winter landscapes with charcoal and graphite on paper. The different qualities of line, which create rhythm and interest in a drawing, are here interpreted in the oxidised silver wire, manipulated into a series of randomly interlocking circles (43). The body acts as a moving canvas across which these lines flow and loop, like the moving of branches against a window pane.

The Dutch artist Onno Boekhoudt also tries to capture the spontaneity of the drawing process with a series of steel wire brooches. Static the pieces have the vitality of a good drawing, in motion there is an imaginative interplay between the moving line and the moving body.

Another English jeweller, Susan May, uses forging techniques to create three-dimensional silver drawings (44). The process of forging helps create the energy and movement of the final form. The dynamic circular structures

43 **Cynthia Cousens**
Density Neckpiece 1996
Oxidised silver, 960mm
NMS Collection

44 **Susan May**
Ring 1996
Silver, 18ct gold, 35mm

beautifully enhance the moving body.

Scottish jeweller Anna Gordon draws oxidised silver and gold wire to fine lengths which are then very carefully composed into brooches and necklaces. These often consist of one dominant drawn element — such as a circle or square — in which other, free hanging geometric elements are contained (45). The formal, essentially linear structure, provides an interesting counterpoint to the volume of the body, like marks on the surface of a sculpted form.

Annelies Planteydt, the Dutch jeweller, also plays with the placing of essentially linear elements against the volume of the body. She uses 18ct gold and tantalum wire to create series of different, asymmetric elements which are then composed into neckpieces. The Double Life Necklace (46) continues a long tradition of the chain as a type of jewellery, but works with the elements — both in shape and colour — in subtle ways to create visual interest, intensified by the movement of the body.

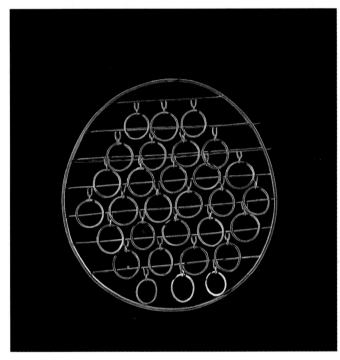

45 **Anna Gordon**
Brooch 1995
Silver, gold, 111×107mm
NMS Collection

46 **Annelies Planteydt**
Double Life Necklace 1996
18ct gold, tantalum, 290mm

PATTERN

Here such a pattern is,
As stretcheth me apart

EDNA ST VINCENT MILLAY

It can be difficult to achieve balanced composition and pattern in small scale objects. On the one hand there is the demand of distilling ideas onto a tiny surface, on the other there is the demand to create pattern which has impact at a distance: the way the work will often be seen.

Japanese artist Suo Emiko applies platinum and gold leaf to bold stainless steel wire structures. The leaf pattern of her necklace (47) reflects light when the piece is being worn, creating a sense of movement across the surface of the piece. Italian artist Stefano Marchetti uses the Japanese *mokume* technique with oxidised silver and gold to build up mosaic-like blocks, which echo the rich patterns of Byzantine art. The

47 **Suo Emiko**
Necklace 1995
Stainless steel, gold leaf,
360×360×125mm

48 Stefano Marchetti
Concave Brooch I 1996/7
Gold, oxidised silver, 55×55mm

blocks are cut into thin sheets, with the resulting elements being re-assembled into the final form (48). Both Emiko and Marchetti create surface patterns which are strikingly effective at a distance, and have the exquisite detail of the miniature when viewed closely.

Another Italian, Giovanni Corvaja, uses both granulation and fine drawn gold threads to compose his brooches. His mastery of these decorative techniques results in structures (49) which are lively and expressive with exquisite tone and textural detail.

Scottish jeweller Graham Crimmins and Swiss artist Carole Guinard both build up shapes and patterns across a canvas of whitened silver (50, 51). Guinard is concerned with producing minute variations on a theme, by placing identical geometric gold shapes, in different combinations, on the silver sheet. A more random pattern emerges in Crimmins' work, in which silver, copper and gold elements are fused onto the silver sheet, to create tiny, lyrical paintings in metal.

50 Carole Guinard
Brooch 1996
Silver, gold, 50×50mm

49 Giovanni Corvaja
Brooch 1997
22ct gold, 55mm dia

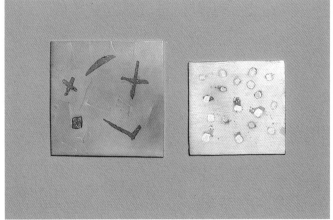

51 Graham Crimmins
Brooches 1994
Silver, fine silver, copper, gold, 50×50mm

SCALE

*To go for giantism
is to go for
self-destruction*

ERNST SCHUMACHER

As Oppi Untracht says, 'it is a tribute to the skill of jewellers that such a diversity of expression can be achieved in relatively small scale objects'. But is small beautiful? Can small be serious as well as decorative? There has been a tendency in the post-war arts to value the big: the big idea; the big installation; the grand gesture: modern museums are filled with paintings and sculpture that fiercely deny the domestic in scale as well as in content. Such attitudes may have freed art from the constraints of the gilt frame, but they have also fostered a certain ignorance about scale.

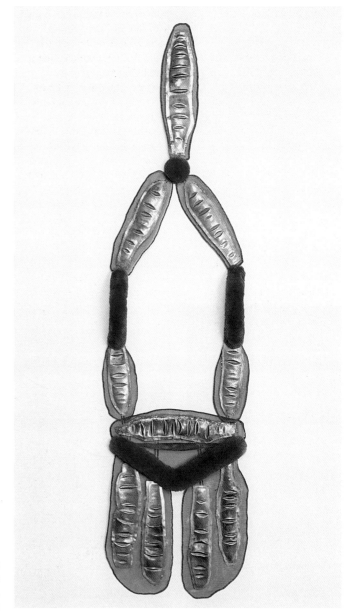

52 **Imke Jörns**
Adornment for the Body 1993
Brass, synthetic fur, wire gauze,
800×300mm

Nobody would deny the power of a Japanese netsuke or a Tassie cameo to convey quite powerful ideas about the human condition, and yet both only measure a few centimetres.

The human body is the scale, the measure, for the size of a piece of jewellery as well as for its form. Ideas of acceptable scale are of course culturally determined: what is acceptable as a Naga head ornament may be challengingly radical in a Glasgow bar (particularly if worn by a man). Work which addresses the possibilities of scale is a recurring theme in studio jewellery and reminds us that scale is an important

but relative value. The jewellers included in this section all consider scale in some detail before creating a work. Although this would be true of most of the makers in this book, the preoccupation with scale is more self-conscious in these examples.

Imke Jörns is a young German artist. Her neckpieces and body pieces, constructed from a range of materials including brass and fur (52), play with the theme of acceptable scale in jewellery. Her materials are all light in weight, so even relatively large structures for the body are complementary rather than dominant. For her the relationship with the wearer is

crucial: she sees the play with scale as a way of reconstructing imaginative relationships between ornament and form. Works for the wearer are tactile and sensuous as well as being ambitious in scale.

Marjorie Schick also explores notions of scale with her elaborate and colourful collars and cuffs (see p23). Schick was an active American member of the New Jewellery Movement in the 1970s: for her the exploration of new materials in jewellery and experimentation with scale were important ways of creating a new language for jewellery. Unlike some of her contemporaries she has never lost sight of the essential

relationship of jewellery to the human body and, like Jörns, she uses lightweight materials such as papier mâché which sit comfortably against the human frame. The generous proportions of the work create a ceremonial, celebratory mood which enhances but does not dominate the wearer.

An intense love of the miniature is present in many cultures, in miniature paintings, dolls' house furniture, netsuke and countless other tiny artworks. Scottish jeweller Grainne Morton is one of the few jewellers who makes specific reference to the very small. Her brooches (53) collect together a series of tiny trophies — flower petals, letters of the alphabet, doll's-house scale representations of familiar objects — and hang them in copper boxes sealed with perspex. Through this scaling down of familiar objects and the valuing of the tiny, Morton cleverly plays on our notions of the treasured and the valued.

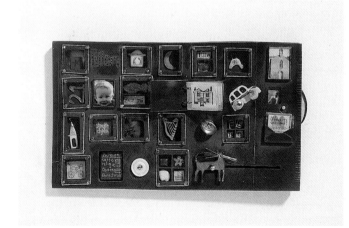

53 **Grainne Morton**
Ellen's 21st
Brooch 1996
Copper, enamel, silver, brass,
found objects, perspex,
65×120mm

STRUCTURE

*Creative engineering...
the rhythmic organisation
of space*
HERBERT READ

Structure refers to the organization of parts into a coherent whole. Different three-dimensional elements can be combined in imaginative and original ways to create powerful final structures. Jewellery structuralists enjoy the additional possibilities for invention in making such structures wearable.

The Catalan artist Xavier Domenech fabricates dynamic structures from silver wire. He works extensively with the brooch form (54) articulating different physical spaces — vessel, house, street — to create a dialogue with the wearer about a sense of place and value. Austrian jeweller Fritz Maierhofer also uses the structures of the built environment as inspiration. In a recent series of rings (55) Maierhofer constructs a series of intersecting planes of metal which can be moved one against the other to create different spaces for the finger. His fascination with structures is balanced by the playfulness of this concept.

Danish artists Karen Ihle and Jens Eliasen, Danish artist Thorkild Thøgersen and English artist Esther Ward work with the formal interplay of identical metal elements to create rhythm and interest in their jewellery. In Ihle/

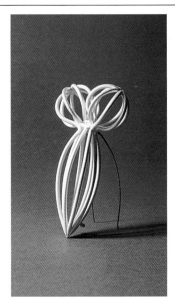

54 **Xavier Domenech**
Brooch 1997
Silver, 80mm

55 **Fritz Maierhofer**
Ring 1997
Stainless steel, 40×24mm

Eliasen's work silver rod is coloured to shades of black and brown to explore the interplay of light and shadow in a structure (56). Thorkild Thøgersen builds up his jewellery from silver wire, either polished or blackened, while Ward exercises a similar technique using stainless steel wire. The artists use the tensile qualities of the metal to help create the final form and the way it moves on the body (57, 58). The concern for creating flexible metal structures is shared by German artist Alexandra Bahlmann (59).

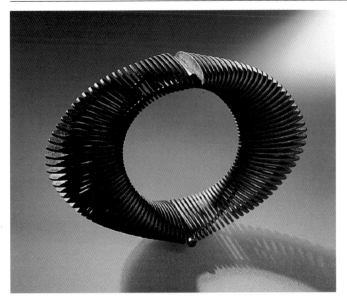

57 **Thorkild Thøgersen**
Necklace 1997
Oxidised silver, 260mm

56 **Karen Ihle/Jens Eliasen**
Bracelet 1996
Coloured silver,
86×130×40mm

59 **Alexandra Bahlmann**
Chain 1994
Tombak, pearls,
500×25×25 mm

58 **Esther Ward**
Ribbon Neckpiece 1993
Stainless steel, 300mm

Scottish jeweller Anne Finlay shows a similar interest in jewellery pared down to integral structural elements. She adds screen printed PVC sheet to the stainless steel wire which also introduces pattern and colour into the work (60). Ann Marie Shillito, another Scottish artist, explores structure through a variety of different forms, inspired by an interest in modern processes such as laser cutting and software design programmes on computer. Shillito's structures (61) are largely determined by this interest in process. Another Scottish maker, Mark Powell, enjoys

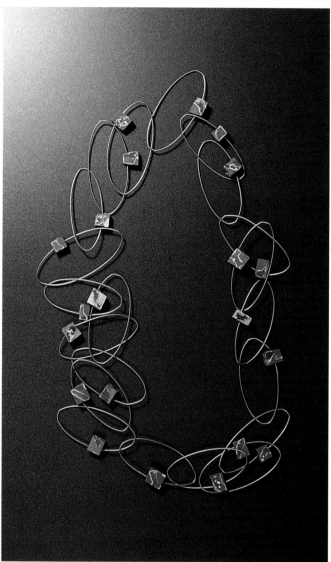

60 **Anne Finlay**
Brooch 1997
Handpainted
PVC, acrylic,
stainless steel,
rubber,
110×185mm

61 **Ann Marie Shillito**
Neckchain 1997
Titanium, aluminium, 380×220mm

exploring the talismanic qualities of certain traditional jewellery structures. He uses intersecting plates of silver and gold, riveted together to create powerful ceremonial neckpieces (62).

Czech artist Jiři Šibor and Slovak artist Anton Cepka both explore metal structures. Šibor cuts, drills and rivets stainless steel using its flexibility and strength to create dynamic forms in combination with glass and plastics (63). Cepka fabricates silver wire in geometric compositions suggestive of machines and industrial components, yet retaining the magical power of jewellery (64).

63 **Jiři Šibor**
Brooch 1997
Stainless steel 85×15×15 mm

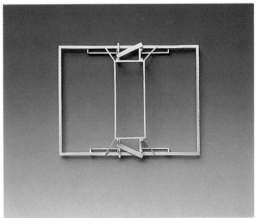

64 **Anton Cepka**
Brooch 1995
Silver, 90×70mm

62 **Mark Powell**
Dragon's tail
Necklace 1997 Gold, 180mm dia

Czech-born, Austrian-based, jeweller Peter Dvorak creates series of elaborately interlocking forms in precious metals. Each piece is carefully worked out through card models, to get precise solutions to the complex angles and relationships in the finished work (65).

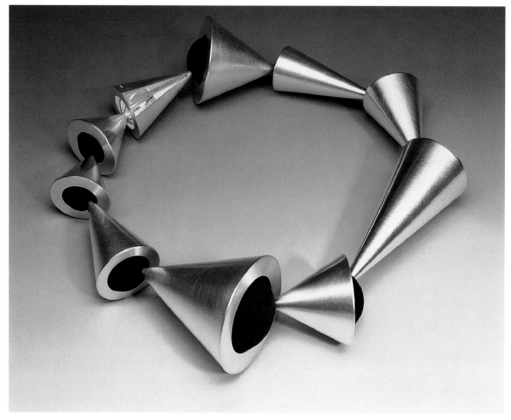

65 **Peter Dvorak**
Funnel Neckpiece 1997
Silver, rubber, 540×180 mm

VOLUME

*The sculptor must feel...
the particular demands
for volume and mass.
The smaller the sculpture,
the more the essentials of
form must exist*

HENRI MATISSE

Jewellery acquires volume in relationship to the body. Some pieces of jewellery, however, use particular qualities of mass and solid form to create effects and express different ideas.

American jeweller Sandra Enterline forms simple, hollow objects from silver which are then coloured and pierced. These objects are containers, often of natural materials, such as wood or preserved insects, and the piercing of the container allows glimpses of the form within. The objects are usually suspended on stainless steel neck wires (66). Enterline uses the tactility of her

sculptural objects to encourage handling and close viewing, which in turn reveals the hidden element within.

Another American, Lisa Spiros, also uses simple three-dimensional forms. Her stainless steel cylinders and cubes are suspended on neck wires creating powerful

jewellery with a distinctively modern aesthetic. The steel is sometimes patinated using oil (67) or chemically whitened to achieve a certain tonal range, but with all her works it is the modulation of three dimensional forms, on a small scale, that gives the work impact.

66 **Sandra Enterline**
Star Fruit Pendant (detail) 1997
Patinated silver, steel, 85×30×30mm

67 **Lisa Spiros**
Pendant 1997
Stainless steel, oil patina, 79×76×16mm

68 Gordon Lawrie
Brooch 1996
Silver, gold, 62×40×12mm

Gordon Lawrie is inspired by the sculptural forms of architecture. His brooches (68) are hammered out of silver sheet and then shaped into a range of small-scale forms inspired by buildings in New Mexico, where he lives and works. The interplay between line, volume, angle and plane is emphasised by the play of light across the hammered surface of the metal and gives the works an inviting three-dimensional presence.

Welsh artist Gavin Fraser-Williams uses solid blocks of metal — whether computer milled steel, or hand raised gold — to create work of an uncompromisingly monumental quality. Although pieces are relatively small scale (69), they express a dominant, massive quality which attracts attention. On closer examination, the fine detail of tone and construction can be enjoyed.

Giampaolo Babetto, the Italian jeweller, is a master of scale and proportion. His gold jewellery epitomises the formal significance which can be achieved with modern studio jewellery. An architect of the small scale, Babetto modulates angle, plane, volume, surface tone and texture, to create some of the most beautiful and wearable jewellery of our times which has all the resonance of large-scale sculpture (70).

A former pupil of Babetto's is the German artist Rudolf Bott. Bott has dedicated over twelve years to training as a jeweller and metalsmith. His formidable metalcraft is realised in a series of jewels which are formally simple but never banal. By subtle detail in the line, edge and combinations of shape, Bott creates jewellery (71) which seems to echo the power of early gold work while retaining a quintessentially modernist aesthetic.

71 Rudolf Bott
Brooch 1996
Gold, 106×35mm

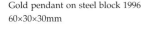

69 Gavin Fraser-Williams
Gold pendant on steel block 1996
60×30×30mm

70 Giampaolo Babetto
Ring 1995
18ct white gold, blue pigment,
35×34×35mm

IDEA & IMAGE

Esther, Comedienne *Earrings, Esther Ward*

*Look into the ashes of a fire, or clouds, or mud ...
you may find really marvellous ideas*

LEONARDO DA VINCI

Idea is inextricably linked with material and form, but for some jewellers the desire to convey a particular idea or meaning, often through symbolic or figurative imagery, can be the overriding motivation. It is worth remembering that whatever the intention of the artist in creating a piece of jewellery it will acquire different values and meanings when seen and when owned and worn. Jewellery for the owner and wearer may have a particular sentimental value, as with a wedding ring or christening jewel, which may be independent of or additional to the maker's original intentions.

Images used and ideas explored in studio jewellery are often influenced by the dual life of a piece of jewellery: as a personally valued object kept in a private house and as something pinned to a body moving around in the outside world. This public/private life of a jewel, (unlike a painting in a private house, say, which is only seen by a chosen circle of people) means that jewellery is at least some of the time a public art. It makes contact with a random group of people who may be in turn intrigued or repelled by it.

FANTASY

If a man were robbed of his fantasies, what pleasure would be left him?

BERNARD LE BOVIER DE FONTENELLE

Fantasy conjures up images of pleasure, excitement, imagination and humour with elements of the surreal and the unexpected. Fantasy is also about the unreal - when we talk of somebody having a rich fantasy life, we are referring to somebody who is not always thinking of or relating to the real world. Fantasy is a form of escapism, a retreat. Fantasy jewels are jewels from another world.

English jeweller Dawn Emms creates a natural fantasy world in cellulose acetate. Her images of strange plants and animals (72) follow a tradition of fantasy jewels going back to the Renaissance, but the work is given a modern twist with the laminated and cast cellulose acetate. London-based jeweller Katy Hackney uses cellulose acetate to create bold, organic forms which are both tactile and fantastic. Underlying her work, like Emms', there is a sense of other worldliness, as in her Propeller necklace, in which she moulds multicoloured cellulose propellers to create a vast

ceremonial necklace which is, rather literally, a flight of fantasy.

Catalan artist Xavier Ines Monclús creates fantastic pictures by placing everyday objects in surreal scenes. In *Cheese Mobile Wagon* and *Spring on Wheels* he plays with the meaning of words and things, and the brooches he creates such as *El Refugi del cel Winter* (73) are playful and imaginative. Play is indeed an essential element of wearing jewellery. Many of us fiddle with earrings, play with necklaces or rotate bangles as we wear them. Monclus cleverly exploits the pleasure of play with his fantasy objects.

German artist Anette Wohlleber uses her skill as a metalworker to build up fantastic images such as the *Zirkuswagen Brooch* (74). Forms are ambiguous, humorous, surreal and, by altering the surfaces of metal, the artist finds a metaphor for change and decay. Irish artist Alan Ardiff also builds pictures in metal, but in his case figurative scenes from domestic life are as likely to dominate, as *In the Bath* brooch (75). The effect is humorous and fun but there is also the aptness of a domestic image for a jewel, which has, in part, a very domestic, very private life.

Carol, Photographer
Necklace, Mark Powell

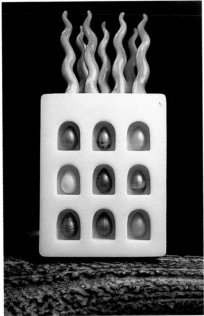

74 Anette Wohlleber
Zirkuswagen Brooch 1995
Silver, lapis lazuli, citrine, enamel

72 Dawn Emms
Bird Box Brooch 1996
Cellulose acetate,
140×75×45mm

73 Xavier Ines Monclús
'El Refugi del cel Winter'
Brooch 1995
Silver, alpaca, wood, 57×55mm

75 Alan Ardiff
In the Bath
Brooch on stand, 1997
Silver, copper, gold, 55×80mm

IDENTITY

*The extreme questions
of contemporary life, questions
of freedom and identity*

JUNE JORDAN

Feelings of personal, cultural and social identity can be destabilised by dramatic social change, as experienced in the late twentieth century. Jewellery is in many ways the ideal art form in which to consider anxieties about identity. People acquire and wear jewellery to illustrate identity. Jewellers make work to establish identity: their identity as a creative person. Knowledge of the lives and identities of different cultures is often read through jewellery.

Identity, our sense of ourselves and others as unique yet interconnected, is essential to our mental health and stability. Current revolt against scientific advances in genetics, for example, is based on our anxieties about identity. An identity crisis suggests a disintegration or a destruction leading to a void. Memory, friendship, love, work and leisure activities all help to build our identities. The ways we speak, move and adorn ourselves all express aspects of our identity.

For Scottish artist Jack Cunningham and Korean artist Eun-Mee Chung jewellery is a way of exploring identity through a sense of place. In Cunningham's work carved stones, charms, and found objects are suspended in flat sheet silver box constructions. The objects are glimpsed as through windows in a house, or through a viewing screen.

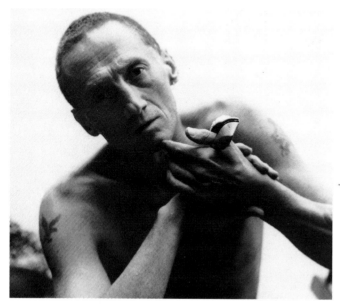

Chris, Actor
Ring, Peter Chang

The elements contained in the brooches are all elements of personal value to the artist — tangible memories of places visited, people known — and the gathered objects create a sense of place in a similar way that, say, collecting shells from the seashore can. They are also arranged to provide colour, texture and contrast within the highly polished silver forms and move within the structure when the brooch is worn. Pieces are titled to guide the viewer towards a meaning (76), but in the end the jewel will acquire different meanings and a different identity with the new owner.

Eun-Mee Chung was born in Korea but has studied and lived for many years in America. Her brooches, constructed from silver, coral and wood, use images drawn from Korean folk craft traditions — such as the *Soté*, a type of totem pole commonly erected outside Korean villages to welcome strangers — to examine questions of identity and belonging (77). Traditional Korean artefacts, like the *Soté*, have often been rejected in the rush to modernise. In such a way important cultural traditions, and hence identities, may become lost to a culture.

Yet at the same time traditional values, in Korea, as much as elsewhere in the world, may have subjugated or undermined certain groups. Traditional values, for many women, in many societies, can mean subjugation to patriarchal systems. Eun-Mee also uses images of enclosed 'female' forms in her work to explore her status as a woman in different cultures.

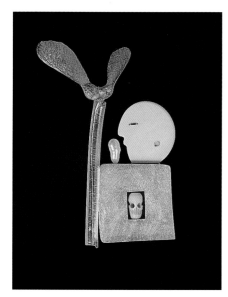

76 Jack Cunningham
Out of the Box
Brooch, 1997
Silver, bone, goldplated sycamore seeds, pearl, 18ct gold, 60×95mm

77 Eun-Mee Chung
Brooch *Soté* Series 1997
Silver, black coral, gold leaf, 120×40mm

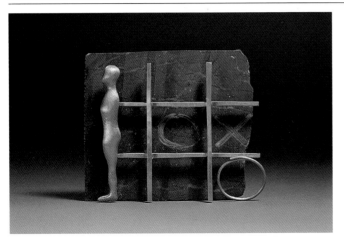

78 Jung-Hoo Kim
The OX Game
Brooch 1996
Silver, local stone, 24ct gold foil,
67×80mm

79 Bruce Metcalf
Illumination Pin 1993
Silver, wood, plastics, gold, 99×75mm

Both American artist Bruce Metcalf and Korean artist Jung-Hoo Kim use figurative imagery to reflect on more general ideas of human identity. These artists use exquisite craftsmanship to construct low-relief images in which human or human-like figures are shown in relationship to a landscape or place. Jung-Hoo Kim forms miniature figures from silver, which are then embellished with 24ct gold foil, using the traditional Korean *keumboo* technique. Local stones, such as lapis and redstone, are used as the backdrop against which these figures are placed and metal is inlaid into the surface of the stone, or laid across it to create the finished image. The tiny figures in her brooches (78) appear to be gazing into infinity, creating a powerful sense of vulnerability and lost identity. Bruce Metcalf fabricates single semi-grotesque figures which seem to be struggling in an unfamiliar world. His work (79) acts as a metaphor for the artist's struggle for identity.

Petteri Ikonen from Finland and Warwick Freeman from New Zealand select materials and symbols which have a particular identity to explore similar issues. Ikonen's use of materials, such as coal and rusting iron, which have a past identity or memory, allows her to consider these questions in wearing jewellery (80). Freeman uses universal symbols: the heart, the star, the flower, fashioned from traditional New Zealand materials, including shell and greenstone, to create brooches which are simultaneously familiar and strange and highlight questions of cultural identity (81).

Vered Kaminski, the Israeli artist, sees identity as a complex issue. To create her brooches she begins by assembling fragments of building stone taken from the streets of Jerusalem. Some of these fragments are made into final pieces of jewellery, others are cast in silver, and the cast silver elements then soldered to create the final piece (82). Kaminski repeatedly re-assembles the same elements to create new brooches which, although different, share a common genetic identity.

New Zealand artist Areta Wilkinson also reflects on cultural identity. Her ancestry is traced through both Maori and *pakeha* (non-Polynesian) culture, and she creates a series of pendants out of shell, bone and other traditional materials which examine identity. The pendants are constructed like museum labels, or identity tags (83), with fragments of numbers and letters. By wearing these the owner actively participates in a discussion about how artefacts from different cultures are seen and collected.

81 Warwick Freeman
Bulb Brooch 1997
Clamshell, basalt, silver, 47×37mm

82 Vered Kaminski
Brooch 1997
Silver, 45×45mm

83 Areta Wilkinson
Bundle 1997
24ct gold, oyster shell, string, 13×23mm

80 **Petteri Ikonen**
Brooch 1995
Red soil, iron, wood coal, goldleaf, 150×40×20mm

INVERSION

*A radical is a man with both feet
planted firmly in the air*

FRANKLIN D ROOSEVELT

Jewellery can be used to question certain ideas as well as to confirm them. This interest in challenging an established order is part of the cycle of creation for most arts. What is evident in much studio jewellery is that the interest often lies in exploring the very nature of jewellery itself.

German artist Karl Fritsch creates jewellery which reflects on the role and meaning of jewellery in people's lives. This jewellery metalanguage (jewellery talking about the nature of jewellery) focuses on the debate about why we wear jewellery at all. Fritsch takes jewellery which has been broken or damaged and 'mends' it by freely modelling random forms in wax to join the broken pieces. These forms are then made permanent by being cast in gold, creating a new work which still retains the memory of the original piece. The Pointy ring (85), shows how the apparently incongruous combination of a free-modelled wax shape and a formal wedding band can result in a work which is visually interesting and simultaneously makes a perceptive comment on the role of jewellery in our lives.

Dutch jeweller Dinie Besems works with a wide range of materials and processes to examine concepts behind jewellery. The 'Portrait of a Perfect Stranger' pendants (86) highlight the role of jewellery in establishing an individual's identity and shows how this can create illusions and be misleading as well as revealing. Besems' other works include a bottle of pheromones

84 **Simon Fraser**
Street Scene, London 1997

and an applicator: the jewel here symbolised as the essence of physical, sexual attraction.

London jeweller Simon Fraser enjoys the theatrical, demonstrative role of jewellery, and recent works have been biased towards performance. A recent project involved him in deconstructing a grand piano over twenty-four hours and making it into jewellery. Although he never loses sight of the body and the wearable object, he is prepared to extend the definition of jewellery to include all the spaces in which it can be seen. He makes intelligent reference to the participatory nature of jewellery — it is seen, worn and enjoyed by a vast range of people and the art of performance is thus a suitable medium in which to celebrate it (84).

Dutch jeweller Onno Boekhoudt celebrates the intuitive process of making as a way of producing imaginative and individual jewellery. His originality rests in the way he can invest the simplest, most unlikely forms with talismanic qualities. His recent work (87) seems to have an affinity with folk or outsider art, with a mixture of naiveté and the direct emotional power of the image.

85 **Karl Fritsch**
Ring 1995
Gold, 50mm

86 **Dinie Besems**
Portrait of a Perfect Stranger
Pendant 1996 Chromed metal, 45×35mm

87 **Onno Boekhoudt**
Room for a Finger 1997
Wood, paint, 40mm

MYTH

*There was a myth before
the myth began*

Wallace Stevens

Myths are invented stories with veiled meanings which tell us something about our society. Myths exist in most cultures and can be traditional, having been handed down through generations, or contemporary, invented to illustrate a particular quality of modern life. Artists often use mythological imagery as a way of expressing certain ideas in a succinct and easily recognisable form.

English jeweller Kevin Coates draws on a range of traditional myths and stories to create his elaborate gold and enamel jewels. He has a parallel career as a musician and inspiration for his work is often drawn from stories associated with music. He starts with a single image and then chooses the most appropriate materials to develop the image into a piece of jewellery. He uses a wide range of techniques, including ones he has invented himself, such as casting gold around and through steel and refractory metals. The Five Towers framed brooch (88) is imagined as a fragment from a lost work demonstrating the mysteries of architecture. Like a myth the fragment acts as a clue to further, hidden meanings.

Ramon Puig Cuyàs, the Catalan artist, is inspired by

Fifi, Actress
Neckpiece, Wendy Ramshaw

traditional myths, particularly those associated with the sea. Unlike Coates, he does not interpret the myth in elaborate figurative pieces, but uses the stories as inspiration for a series of lively abstract brooches. Vigorous drawn lines in metal are animated against a backdrop of brilliant blocks of colour — often pigment on copper or paper as in the *Archipelago* brooch (89).

Catalan-based, Scottish-born, artist Judy McCaig is inspired by the myths and legends of different cultures. Her tiny, low-relief brooches, such as *The Stalking Moon* brooch (90), are built up by chasing, etching and repoussé on copper and silver. The metal is coloured to dark tones of grey with highlights of gold leaf or inlaid gold. McCaig also carves and paints wooden boxes to contain the brooches, which emphasise ideas of preciousness and fragility. All her work uses images of animals, which are shown on quests or journeys through strange landscapes. The work has the mysterious allegorical quality of ancient legends.

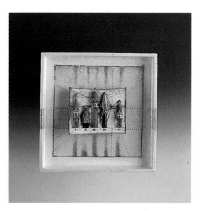

88 Kevin Coates
Five Towers
Brooch in frame 1995
Gold, silver, coral, emerald, aquamarine, tourmaline, bone, wood, paint, gold leaf, 57.5×71.5mm

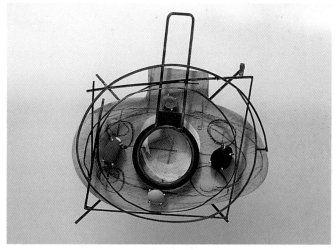

89 **Ramon Puig Cuyàs**
Archipelago
Brooch 1997
Silver, nickel, wood, stones, 90×90×18mm

90 **Judy McCaig**
The Stalking Moon
Brooch in Box 1993
Silver, gold, brass, diamond, ruby, emerald, wood, 55×35mm (brooch)

Scottish jeweller Eileen Gatt also uses animal imagery to explore ancient stories associated with the sea. She is interested in the tension between traditional patterns of life and folklore and the contemporary world and her cast or formed animals are often shown suspended in resin or in metal frames — like gallery or museum exhibits.

Japanese jeweller Sunao Sera uses chemically-coloured copper and painted enamel to create her decorative, symbolic jewellery (91). She enjoys the challenge of producing poetic and personal work out of an essentially unyielding and cold material such as metal. Pieces often incorporate fragments of paper and silk which hint at further meanings, veiled, allusive and incomplete.

91 **Sunao Sera**
Brooches 1997
Copper, brass, paper, silver, enamel, 110x55mm/90x50mm

NATURE

Gie me ae spark o' Nature's fire,
That's a' the learning I desire

ROBERT BURNS

Inspiration from landscape can be shown in many ways: in the forms used, in particular images or colours drawn from the natural world, or in the materials collected in different landscapes which are constructed into the finished piece. Such materials may be selected for decorative qualities and the sense of place they evoke. For others the evocation of the natural world, by

whatever means, is a way of creating awareness of its beauty but also that this beauty is under threat.

Dutch artist Laura Bakker creates delicate necklaces and bracelets by hammering and forging gold and copper wires. By using the action of different pliers she builds up rhythmic shapes — spiral, zigzag, curve — which are then combined with beachcombings, such as

sea shells and sea glass, to create the finished piece. The original inspiration for the work stems from a period spent living in coastal Thailand, where she had few tools or materials. The Seashells necklace (92) shows her confident ability to create interesting forms through these simple techniques.

Senada, Sculptress
Necklace, Cynthia Cousens

93 **Elisabeth Holder**
Rings for Twigs 1997
Palladium, silver, found materials,
8.5×21×34.5mm

92 **Laura Bakker**
At the Tide-line
Necklace (detail) 1993
Tantalum, sea shells, 200×500mm

German jeweller Elisabeth Holder is predominantly known for her technically sophisticated and austere silver and steel jewellery. Recent work such as *Rings for Twigs* (93) develops her interest in form by combining fabricated metal elements with found materials. The metal circles are fashioned to create a clip-like structure into which different objects can be inserted. The combination of rigid structure and random element is inspired by observation of the natural world and provides an opportunity to celebrate the natural world in the materials of the work itself.

Japanese jeweller Kasuko Mitsushima is fascinated by the fluidity and flexibility of glass. She uses it to explore elements of the natural world and her artist's vision is, in a quintessentially Japanese way, informed by a love and respect for nature. The silver and glass ring shown is entitled *Praying the glaciers on the earth won't melt*. The rough cut glass form is held in place by the tension of the silver: if the glass should break the circle would disintegrate (94).

Scottish-based jeweller Grainne Morton makes extensive use of flower heads and petals in her work (p69). In a recent series of brooches petals are suspended in copper and perspex boxes. Bold and decorative jewellery is created by preserving nature. London-based Swiss jeweller Hans Stofer and American jeweller Sandra Enterline also preserve nature. These artists suspend insects in transparent containers, like specimens in a laboratory, which are then fabricated into pieces of jewellery. Their work echoes a tradition of using insects for decorative purposes in jewellery. However, in these works the insect is preserved as distinct and complete, suggesting a greater reverence for the preciousness and vulnerability of the natural world.

Italian Barbara Paganin and Korean Seung-Hee Kim are both inspired by the rich formal reservoir of the natural world. Seung-Hee Kim celebrates the

94 Kasuko Mitsushima
Ring 1997
Glass, silver, 50×35×23mm

95 Seung-Hee Kim
Bud Brooches 1997
Amber, onyx, silver, 24ct gold,
80×15mm

96 Barbara Paganin
Anemone Rosso
Brooch 1996
Gold, oxidised silver, Venetian beads, 60×40mm

97 Malcolm Appleby
Brooch 1997
Iron, gold, moonstone, 90×50mm

energy of the natural world through a series of brooches inspired by spring and the cycle of renewal. Her Bud brooches (95) are constructed from silver, gold and amber. The forms echo the buds on a spring branch and the materials are selected to reinforce an image of vitality.

Paganin's recent series of brooches, made from gold and Venetian glass beads, are inspired by the underwater world of coral reefs. The Anemone brooches (96) echo their natural counterparts as the gold and glass tentacles gently vibrate with the movement of the body.

Scottish artist Malcolm Appleby celebrates the energy of the natural world in his engraved and fused metal jewellery. An engraver of world-class ability, Appleby is able to harness his technique in ways which suggest the rhythm of water, the vitality of fire and the play of light and shadow across a sunlit landscape (97).

German jeweller Stephan Seyffert also uses the forms of the natural world as an inspiration. However, in his case, these forms are seen as products of man's continued scientific experiment which changes and alters nature. He designs work which imagines materials for the future — giant pearls, renewable coral and stretch crystals (98).

Australian artist Sally Marsland creates series or groups of brooches which celebrate the repetitive but asymmetrical patterns of nature. She casts and lathe-turns aluminium and silver to create tactile, organic pieces (99). Danish artist Per Suntum uses traditional jewellery materials such as precious metals and enamel to celebrate his experience of nature: the shimmering light in a Cretan sea, the textures and tones of a rock-strewn shore. The expressive, organic forms of his recent brooches (100) seem to capture the vitality of the transient experience.

98 **Stephan Seyffert**
Stretch Crystal
Necklace 1996
Silicon rubber, 230mm

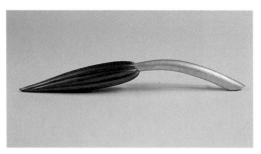

99 **Sally Marsland**
Brooch 1996
Silver, anodised aluminium,
130×11×16mm

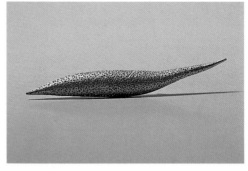

100 **Per Suntum**
Yquem Brooch 1997
Silver, gold, steel, 116×16×10mm

POLITICS

'Beauty' is a currency like the gold standard. Like any economy it is determined by politics.

NAOMI WOLF

The public nature of jewellery can make it a particularly suitable medium for political comment. A stimulating exhibition at the Crafts Council, London, in 1995, entitled *What is Jewellery?* included a section devoted to all the different badges and symbols that we pin to our coats to signify sympathy with, or allegiance to, a particular cause: the red ribbon, the poppy, the red rose (in Britain a symbol for the Labour Party).

Every aspect of our dress is to some extent a political act: that we choose to wear historic jewels, say, rather than contemporary work, may indicate something about our attitude to tradition and innovation.

Israeli jeweller Esther Knobel takes forms, such as the medal, which have strong symbolic associations with warfare. Working in an often turbulent political arena, Knobel is influenced by the

idea of dress and ornamentation as anything but innocent and frivolous. Her childlike faces, imprinted on the surface of the medal, remind us of the innocents who often suffer from a glorification of war (101).

Australian artist Helen Britton creates jewellery concerned with environmental issues. Her selection of industrial waste materials, particularly plastics, comments on the waste and

Frank, Dancer
Brooch, Esther Knobel

101 **Esther Knobel**
Medal 1997
Silk, nickel, silver leaf, 90mm

102 **Helen Britton**
Assemblage
Brooch 1997
Plastics, pearls, opal, silver, 50mm

104 **Joyce Scott**
Cold Water Snake
Necklace 1994 Beadwork, thread,
405×300mm

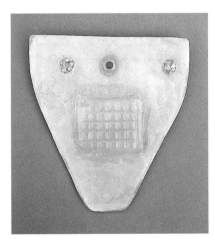

103 **Bussi Buhs**
Garbage Brooch 1997
Silicone, polyester, stone, silver, 85mm

destructiveness of many modern societies. Her sinister, edgy forms evoke strong suggestions of danger and poison — symbolic of environmental pollution (102). German artist Bussi Buhs also uses industrial waste as her principal material. Her *Garbage Jewellery* (103) is underpinned by considerable technical skill in casting, laminating and injection moulding plastic waste into different forms. The sinister images she attains are similarly suggestive of the destructiveness of waste.

Afro-American artist Joyce Scott addresses race and gender issues in her work. She uses a traditional Native American technique of beadwork to create highly coloured glass collars and cuffs (104). Many of the images in her work tell stories of racial violence or sexual harassment. The work is sensuous and enjoyable to wear, but explores serious themes both in the selection of a particular technique and in the images used.

Norwegian jeweller Lillan Eliassen makes striking rings from silver and acrylic (105). All Eliassen's work uses traditional symbols of romance such as hearts and flowers. However, when you clasp the heart or flower the ring opens to reveal a glittering knife. Her work explores a jewellery tradition in which the decorative ring can have hidden menace (think of the Borgias' enthusiasm for poison rings) and also subverts traditional, gendered symbols of romance.

Canadian artist Barbara Stutman also examines gender issues through her jewellery. She selects images from the world of advertising, images in which female beauty is often used to sell luxury goods. She then reconstructs these images using a range of textile techniques with metal wire, into elaborate jewels which ironically subvert the content (106).

Swiss jeweller Sophie Hanagarth creates jewellery in the image of different parts of the body, highlighting the relationship between the jewel and the body, but also, like Stutman, the relationship between the jewel and socially constructed images of femininity. In the necklace illustrated (107), the balls hang directly over the genitalia of the female wearing the work.

105 **Lillan Eliassen**
Heart Carousel
Ring 1996
Plated silver, polyester, marbles, 95×100mm

106 **Barbara Stutman**
Is Hot Stuff Delicious?
Ring/Brooch Sculpture 1997
Magnet wire, silver wire, peppercorns, 50mm×40mm/95mm×30mm

107 **Sophie Hanagarth**
Balls
Necklace 1997
Iron nails, 1650×55×40mm

Australian Fiona Kwong plunders slick, advertising-style images of intimate femininity. She takes images of parts of the body closely associated with sensuality and sexuality and reinterprets them as witty and wearable jewels (108). By refashioning different images of sexuality she asserts the right of women to create sexually adventurous images for themselves.

Dutch artist Felieke van der Leest demonstrates a similarly playful and subversive attitude to gender and wearing jewellery (109). Her imaginative jewellery, in a range of woven fibres and metal wire, makes clever use of simple images to remind us of the link between adornment and sexuality.

108 **Fiona Kwong**
Luscious Lips I
Brooch 1994
Acrylic, silver, rubber, 34×22×8mm

109 **Felieke van der Leest**
Little Pig with Red Boots
Pendant 1996 Woven fibre, 42mm

SYMBOL

A set of wordless symbols, effortlessly shared

JOHN UPDIKE

Jewellery can be a political symbol, and certain universal symbols such as the heart, circle and fish can be adopted or subverted to create different identities. The language of art is of course a language of symbols — those two flat strokes of paint symbolise a tree, those two lumps of clay a human torso. Jewellery, in whatever form, is in itself a symbol: a symbol of power, wealth, sexuality and certain social customs.

French-born, Australian jeweller Pierre Cavalan has been described as a 'poet of recent archaeology'. What he is excavating is the meaning contained in modern emblems like institutional insignia, badges, and other club ephemera. He places these items in a traditional jewel-like framework fabricated from silver, gold and semi-precious stones to make elegant, opulent jewellery (110). Although assemblage for ironic effect is a

common artistic device, Cavalan's impeccable skill with materials and stylish composition creates original and powerful jewellery.

Catalan artist Joaquim Capdevila is similarly skilful as a jeweller. He comes from a long-established jewellery family in Barcelona, which underpins his ability to use a wide range of materials. A recent body of work has explored the tree as a symbol of life. Simple representations of

Marlyn, Student
Brooch, Grainne Morton

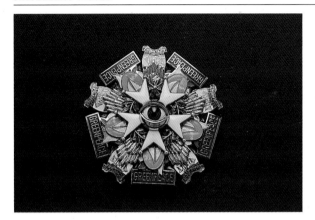

110 **Pierre Cavalan**
Rainbow Warrior Medal 1995
Silver, found objects, 70×70×15mm

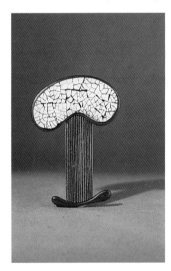

111 **Joaquim Capdevila**
Trees
Brooch 1997
Gold, lacquer, eggshell, 65×50mm

trees are meticulously constructed from silver and gold with brilliant colours and contrast added through the application of layers of Japanese lacquer (111).

Swedish jeweller Christer Jonsson constructs brooches out of a succession of symbols made from different materials (112). The rich symbolism of European baroque jewels is an inspiration: recurring motifs of the skull, the heart, the flower are suggestive of the alchemist's workshops. Jonsson's skilful use of colour and symbol results in tiny carnival pieces, which reflect on eternal themes of human life and destiny.

112 **Christer Jonsson**
Cupidos Garden
Brooch 1995
Gilded silver, titanium, agate, enamel, 130mm

Australian artist Carlier Makigawa employs a range of symbols such as flower, flame and trefoil, commonly used in both oriental and western cultures. The cast resin symbols are contained within a silver wire structure the shape of which echoes the form of the resin object and acts as protection or definition for it. Pendants are designed to hang over the stomach area of the wearer: the area of the body traditionally associated with energy in eastern philosophies such as Tai Chi. By emphasising this part of the body the pendants symbolise the energy of the wearer (113).

113 **Carlier Makigawa**
Pendant 1997
Monel, silver, resin, silk, 460mm

Scottish artist Geoff Roberts uses the symbol of the fish: a symbol widely associated with fertility and abundance in many cultures. In Roberts' work groups of fish are suspended in frames, hang dripping down the side of corsets or climb over the rim of gladiatorial headpieces. It is work which celebrates abundance, excess. All the jewellery is like regalia for a forgotten religion, brilliant, exotic and strange, yet when worn invests the wearer with symbols of ceremonial power (114).

Mah Rana, the English jeweller, takes the gold wedding band — the symbol of the unbroken circle, eternity, — and represents it in a different context. She collects rings from pawnbrokers and refashions them into new jewellery by the addition of other elements or materials. In this way, the pawned ring becomes yet again something lasting, meaningful, loved...or does it? The necklace shown is held together by a slender knot in the base of the silk ribbon, easily untied (115).

114 **Geoff Roberts**
View through a Creel
Belt ornament 1997 Printed leather, welded steel, 230mm

115 **Mah Rana**
I Never Promised You a Rose Garden No 1
Neckpiece 1996
Gold, stainless steel, satin ribbon, 260×205mm
NMS Collection

If Rana reflects on the fragility of symbols of eternity, Hans Stofer revels in taking objects and symbols familiar in one setting and transferring them into another (116). This familiar Dadaist technique of transposed context creates new meanings for and relationships between the wearer, objects and symbols. Here Stofer takes the child's throwaway rubber dummy, reversing its symbolic boy/girl colours and creates a permanent, beautifully crafted steel framework for it. The resulting work is amusing and allows us to reflect on the disposable item now made precious and lasting. There is the added sensual resonance of the dummy as desired object.

116 **Hans Stofer**
Comfort for Boys — Comfort for Girls
Brooches 1997
Mild steel, white paint, plastic, rubber, dental steel, 100×50mm

THE BODY

Susan, Lecturer *Collar, Verena Sieber-Fuchs*

A piece of jewelry, what is it until you relate it to the body?

ART SMITH

So far we have explored studio jewellery in relation to the materials, forms, images and ideas used. Throughout, however, we have continued to emphasise the idea of jewellery being worn, and we now return to this aspect in more detail. In this section, we look at work by jewellers who particularly celebrate the essential physical and sensual pleasure that can be gained from wearing imaginative studio jewellery.

MOVEMENT

Our Nature consists in movement

BLAISE PASCAL

Jewellery moves — inevitably. As soon as you move, so does it. The effect of a piece of jewellery, the way it is seen by the viewer, changes as soon it is worn: the play of light across the surface of metal; the movement of earrings against the frame of the face. Movement gives vitality to all jewellery, both conventional and original. For the wearer of a jewel, movement can provide other pleasurable aspects to the piece: the weight moving against the body, the sound created by different elements moving together, the movement of elements against the skin.

German jeweller Hilde Janich exploits the potential of light and movement in her parchment and gold wire necklaces (117). Slender scraps of parchment are suspended on elaborate wire structures to create necklaces which, when worn, create the illusion of a series of shapes hovering over the body of the wearer. The light catches the wire and the translucent parchment with each movement of the body.

117 **Hilde Janich**
Necklace 1997
Parchment, gold, nylon, 175mm

118 **Sonia Morel**
Ring 1997
Silver, 50mm

Swiss artist Sonia Morel makes 'toys for the hands'. She constructs elaborate structures for the finger onto which freehanging metal elements are suspended (118). In movement these touch and caress the hand of the wearer, and the moving metal traps light and shadow against the skin of the wearer.

American jeweller Rachelle Thiewes builds up elaborate neckpieces and cuffs from simple slate and silver elements. The elements are all freehanging, suspended from the main structure, and move with the movement of the body (119). Thiewes enjoys engaging with this essential, kinetic element of jewellery and designs the pieces to create sound as well as movement: the elements moving together create a sound like the rustling of wind across cactus plants in her native New Mexico.

119 **Rachelle Thiewes**
Necklace 1995
Silver, carved slate, 686mm

SENSUALITY

*Shivering-sweet
to the touch*

FRANCES CORNFORD

Gold has been used universally as a jewellery material, partly due to its sensual possibilities. In the right hands, such as those of British jewellers Daphne Krinos and Susan Cross, its sensual qualities can be enjoyed to the full. Cross solders hundreds of tiny gold rings (120) which are then built up into chains to drape and fold across the body like fabric. In her most recent work, the flexibility of fabric is reproduced in minutely elaborated metal structures.

Krinos hammers and forges gold wire into fluid forms which celebrate the pleasure of wearing. The gold is left with a hammer finish, to create the soft light-absorbing surfaces, which feel warm against the skin and have the resonance of

120 **Susan Cross**
Necklace 1995
18ct gold, 470mm

early Mediterranean gold work (121).

American jeweller Arline Fisch has worked extensively with textile techniques in metal over many years and in recent pieces such as the *Green Waterfall with Fish* necklace

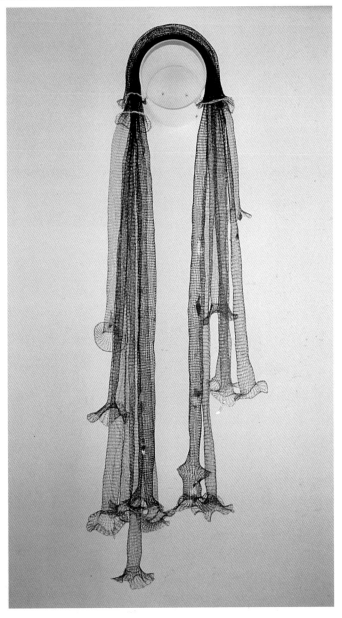

(122) the different woven and knitted elements flow against the body with the seductive rhythm of water. Australian artist Rowena Gough strings together hundreds of pearl buttons, of different sizes, to produce flexible, tactile jewellery which is a delight to handle and wear (p26).

121 **Daphne Krinos**
Earrings/Necklace (detail) 1995
18ct gold, tourmaline, aquamarine,
40×80mm/380mm

122 **Arline Fisch**
Green Waterfall with Fish
Necklace 1996
Silver, copper, 200×1050mm

Norwegian artist Tone Vigeland has for a period of over forty years been concerned with creating sensual jewellery which has the power and presence of sculpture. She typically uses techniques such as chainmail to create jewellery which hangs comfortably over the body and reacts to its movements. Her restrained palette concentrates on the blacks and greys of oxidised silver or steel, sometimes with highlights of gold, and her artist's eye for spatial rhythm ensures the

jewellery has powerful presence (123).

Dutch artist Jacomyn van der Donk uses fibre, flexible metal chain, glass and bone to create her rhythmical and sensual jewellery. Her works celebrate the physical pleasure of wearing a jewel in the way the pieces flow and move with the body. In addition, the sensuality of jewellery wearing is underlined by the inclusion of fragments of photographs, drawn from erotica, within the structure of the jewel (124).

123 **Tone Vigeland**
Bracelet 1995
Silver, 65×68mm

124 **Jacomyn van der Donk**
Necklace 1995
Silver, glass, paper, 195×175×400mm
Museum of Modern Art, Arnhem

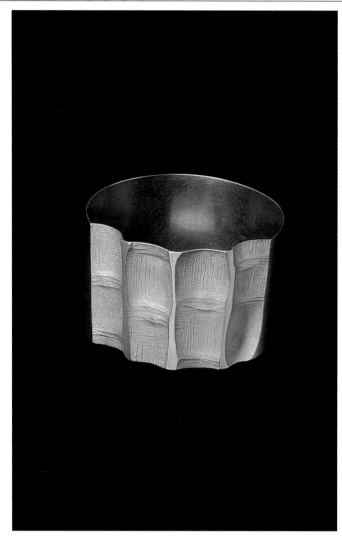

Gerd Rothmann, a German jeweller, takes wax impressions from part of the wearer's body, and casts them into repeating gold elements, which are then constructed into simple neckpieces or bangles (125). The work has an immediate sensual connection with the wearer, since the surface is patterned by their own skin, and the impression of fingers on the surface of the gold reinforces the image of the tactile, sensual and erotic jewel.

Tactility is an important part of wearing and enjoying jewellery. Swiss artist Esther Brinkmann has created a series of *Fingervessels* (126) from hammered metal sheets:

125 **Gerd Rothmann**
Four Finger Bracelet 1995
18ct gold, 68×43mm

silver for colour; gold for malleability and lustre; iron for challenge and hardness. These metal elements are combined with woven silk thread which together form original and tactile rings. The silk element is pushed over the finger and can be used to adjust the position of the ring. The play between the flexible thread and rigid, but tactile, metal gives visual interest and encourages the pleasurable touching of the piece by the wearer.

Katy Hackney also explores tactile rings — rings are after all worn on the part of the body used to experience touch. Tiny silver beads are placed into holes drilled into bold cellulose acetate forms. The acetate/silver elements are often freehanging on ridged silver shanks — the finger holds the form in place, but the ring still moves and encourages touch and play (127).

Dutch artist Beppe Kessler uses short lengths of fabric which are painted, stiffened, twisted and pleated to incorporate stones or found objects. The contrast between the silken surface of the fabric and the weight and shape of the fabric-covered stones sets up immense temptation to touch and handle the piece. By touch, you can discover what it is hard to understand by looking alone (p18).

126 **Esther Brinkmann**
Fingervessel 1995
Silver, textile, 35×55mm

127 **Katy Hackney**
Ring 1996
Silver, cellulose acetate, 30×30×50mm
Crafts Council Collection

STUDIO JEWELLERY IN CONTEXT

Up to this point, we have looked at studio jewellery in relation to its distinctive, individual qualities, the different forms and materials used, and the different ideas expressed. This section considers how those who promote and buy work can influence what is produced. This influence is rarely discussed in relation to any contemporary art, but can be crucial both to the artists themselves and to the status of their work in society.

To some extent, the history of art is the history of patronage. A Cellini salt cellar is as much a product of the taste of its sixteenth-century patron, as a Wendy Ramshaw ringset is the product of its twentieth-century buyer. Shifts in the style and content of works of art have always reflected the changing profile of their collectors and patrons. Thus religious art, art celebrating the material world, and art which anxiously denies its very materiality, can be seen to reflect respectively the patronage of the Church, the Renaissance princes and the wealthy classes of urban society.

The tradition of the supremacy of the artistic individual, the post-Romantic vision of the artist as above the common standard, often ignores this social context. In reality, however visionary the

individual artists, their vision to some extent resides within the culture in which they live. Additionally, the vision may be communicated with the assistance of a range of other individuals and institutions, who may ultimately determine whether the vision is communicated at all.

Contemporary studio jewellery, like all art, is affected by its social context. By considering the role of public galleries, private collectors, private galleries and by highlighting social conventions of wearing jewellery, in the West at least, we can begin to build a picture of the late twentieth-century context for studio jewellery, and how this may affect what is produced.

The public collector

Why do museums and other institutions collect jewellery? The reasons why particular objects enter public collections can sometimes seem mysterious. The underlying premise is that collections are built, and maintained, for and on behalf of all of us. Beyond that premise, every public collection has its own reasons and methods.

Many different types of museum and gallery collect contemporary studio jewellery. Museums devoted solely to

jewellery are very rare (one of the few is the Schmuckmuseum in Pforzheim). Instead, jewellery is collected, to a greater or lesser extent, by institutions concerned more generally with the decorative arts, social history, local history, craft, design, costume, even science and technology: all areas in which jewellery is involved.

If museums are to record significant developments in taste and technology in society, they must add continuously to their collections. Manufactured objects can illustrate social, cultural, political and economic changes within society, and the effect this has on given individuals. Within displays, contemporary jewellery can be used to reflect continuity, or change, in many aspects of daily life from fashion to social rituals and customs. The exhibition of individual achievement is also frequently used to provide inspiration for future makers.

In reality 'institutions' do not collect at all. Collections are assembled by people, sometimes a single curator, often a board. It is rare for a single individual, in a publicly funded institution, to select work on their own; virtually all acquisitions will be vetted and approved by others within or outwith that institution. Every jewellery enthusiast may dream of being allowed to select and collect jewellery at someone else's expense. However there are disadvantages: they cannot wear it and they cannot take it with them when they leave.

In addition, responsibility can weigh heavily on curators who acquire contemporary objects by living artists. The acquisition of a jeweller's work for a public collection is seen by makers as an official seal of approval and by the public as an indicator of excellence. A curator may feel constrained by awareness of this responsibility. It is far easier to collect with the benefit of hindsight (even after, say, ten years) using the test of time, than to collect current work. Knowing that mistakes, as well as successes, will be evident for posterity, can sap the confidence. Perhaps curators are overly concerned. Without the efforts of nineteenth-century curators in collecting what was then contemporary material, our museums would be much poorer interpreters of that century. The contemporary perspective is at least as important as what is acquired.

Museum collecting therefore treads a delicate path. It must recognise it is both active and passive, a market leader and a market follower. At one level it is recording what exists; at another it may stimulate the actual production of work by its patronage.

Public collecting can be very controversial, so questions of accountability are important. In Britain, a written collecting policy is a criterion for museum registration. Curators must understand what their own institutions are trying to achieve and justify their collecting within that context. The published collecting policy should satisfy our right to know what is being done on our behalf, and give the curator an essential tool for making choices.

How does a curator choose? Faced with hundreds of excellent makers, and thousands of pieces of jewellery, how does a curator choose what to buy? The starting point is research, which is carried out wherever studio jewellery appears. This might include visiting exhibitions, jewellery fairs, degree shows, specialist galleries, workshops and colleges; reading books, catalogues and magazines; talking to makers, tutors, other curators, gallery owners and private buyers. It is essential to absorb, to keep track of new developments, to watch what people are buying and wearing. The curator needs to be a kind of human sponge, with a finely honed visual memory.

The next step is ensuring a work relates to the institution's collecting policy. Does the piece meet the agreed criteria, and how might it be used? As an example, in the National Museums of Scotland, jewellery is selected on the basis of technical and/or aesthetic excellence; the use of new materials or new techniques in established materials; the demonstrable influence of the maker on the work of other makers, or on particular developments within the discipline; illumination of particular themes, such as textile techniques in jewellery; or to mark changes in makers' preoccupations (such as recycling of materials).

There are economic factors to be considered. Public collections spend public money and curators must ensure value for money. The National Museums of Scotland, like most museums, purchase from numerous different sources in an attempt to be impartial and responsible. Work may be bought from makers, or from specialist jewellery fairs, but often it comes from private galleries. The private gallery owners will have spent time and effort in selecting good artists, from a wide geographic area, and in selecting good works from those artists. This enables the curator to see and discuss a good range of work in a relatively convenient and efficient way, without having to travel extensively to seek out the best piece. In addition, as a gallery can be an important outlet for many studio jewellers, the encouragement and support given by museum purchases can be significant for all concerned.

Stringent financial considerations in most museums mean that there will be hard decisions to be made and priorities to be set, to ensure the best use of whatever resources are available. For the National Museums of Scotland, where jewellery competes with an extraordinary range of different subject areas for limited purchase funds, this may mean applying for supporting grants, choosing a single piece from a maker rather than a series, and only attempting to illustrate significant changes in an artist's direction, rather than a gradual update. Few curators regret an acquisition, once made: far more common are regrets for the missed opportunities, where pieces have been lost through lack of funds, lack of confidence or the inability to persuade others of the strength of the case.

Collecting personal ornaments for an institution is bittersweet. Once a piece enters a public collection, it will never be used as it was intended — as a wearable object. It becomes subject to the museum's duty of long-term care and conservation, and is rarely handled. Sometimes it seems better to reject a piece of jewellery, because it seems so wrong that it will not be worn. Commissioning of jewellery raises similar issues, as it is difficult to see how a maker can produce something as personal as a piece of jewellery, for something as impersonal as an institution. The National Museums of Scotland choose not to commission unless there is no real alternative.

Not all additions to public collections are purchases. Most museums have limited funds for acquisition, and rely greatly on the generosity of donors. Welcome as they are, donations also carry risks. They can conflict with a carefully thought-out collecting strategy, for instance, or they may come with strings. Like purchases, potential donations need to be fully assessed for appropriateness, if they are to do justice to both the donor and to the public.

It may be several years before the shape of a public collection begins to emerge, but emerge it will; and because collections are made by individuals, all collections have distinctive individual qualities. Such qualities are developed and changed as successive generations of curators leave their mark on the collections, but they nonetheless remain unique to the individual institution.

Responsible collecting by public institutions can bring many positive benefits. By encouraging and illustrating excellence it can provide important support to makers, and be a useful source of information to all its visitors. There are risks. Public collecting of contemporary material can become self-referential, whereby curators draw mutual confidence by following each other's leads. If all museums collect the same things, the public are denied a more representative range of work. Additionally, if the status bestowed on work included in public collections begins to dictate standards of acceptable taste, this could unbalance studio jewellery's most important relationship: that with the individual wearer.

The private collector

One such individual wearer is the private collector. The private collector can have a considerable influence on the development of certain styles of art. In the twentieth century, for instance, well-known collectors of contemporary art, like Charles Saatchi in Britain, can directly affect what receives attention and patronage in the wider market. Even anonymous collectors can be very influential in shaping the kind of work produced, through the simple exercise of informed purchasing power.

Studio jewellery is increasingly benefiting from the attention of the private collector. Although the market remains less developed, in collecting terms, than for some forms of art, a growing number of individuals are recognising the quality and diversity of studio jewellery and are buying it in the consistent and sustained way indicative of a collector. One such individual is Dr Mary Smith, an academic based in Scotland. Over the past fifteen years she has amassed a significant collection of contemporary studio jewellery. The consistency and quality of her collecting make her an interesting case study and offer insights into what qualities an individual collector may be seeking in a piece of studio jewellery.

Dr Smith's collection comprises mainly brooches and neckpieces and is almost exclusively made in metal. There are some forty or fifty pieces in total and most of the work is British. Although all work is bought with the collector's eye for quality, it is also, crucially, bought to be worn, and the types of work Smith chooses are influenced by what she can wear comfortably in most social situations.

In tracing the origin of her interest in contemporary jewellery Smith cites two important influences. The first was her mother, a highly successful surgeon, who taught herself to make jewellery in the Midlands in the 1960s. She did this partly in response to the dearth of contemporary work available; partly in the spirit of the self-reliant culture of the post-war years, when it was considered normal to master a range of skills. The kitchen table became a workbench from which jewellery of considerable precision and imagination evolved. Secondly, Smith has her own long-established interest in well-made, imaginative clothing, and is herself an accomplished dressmaker.

These two aspects of Dr Smith's background underpin important strands in the composition of her collection. Her informed interest in how things are made is reflected in the imaginative quality of the workmanship of collected pieces, and in the emphasis on metalwork. Additionally, her interest in clothing has inspired the acquisition of works which show original approaches to wearability.

Smith describes herself as a 'visual sensualist'. This emphasises both her sense of the importance of the physical character of a piece of jewellery and her belief that a piece of jewellery, like any significant work of art, has to elicit a direct, emotional response from the viewer. As an academic and a collector she values an analytical and intellectual approach to art appreciation, but is also concerned that, in pursuit of pedantry, the fundamental pleasure of seeing and, in the case of jewellery, wearing work of real quality may be lost. For her, jewellery rests on the twin peaks of sensual and intellectual pleasure.

Smith also highlights the enjoyment that can be gained from communicating this pleasure to others. She identifies numerous occasions when the jewellery she has been wearing has attracted interest and enthusiastic appraisal from a range of other individuals: individuals who may otherwise never have been able to see work of real quality being worn. Jewellery collectors can be enlightened and important ambassadors.

Smith's collection could perhaps be classified as fine studio jewellery. The emphasis is on work which is structurally formal, with relatively little additional surface decoration, and tends towards the classically proportioned. Pieces are mostly made from gold, silver or non-precious metals. Stylistically they owe a debt to European modernism, with little evidence of American-style figurative or narrative work. The quality resides in the subtle detail, such as the tone or texture of the surface, or in the way a piece works imaginatively and surprisingly when worn.

Although most of the work is by British makers such as Cynthia Cousens, Gerda Flöckinger, Dorothy Hogg, Jacqueline Mina and Wendy Ramshaw, Smith has not set national boundaries on her collecting. To some extent the content has been determined by what has been available to her in the British market, which all too rarely includes work from other countries. However, she has been able to echo the sensuality and formal rigour of her gold, roller-imprinted Mina pendant in a magnificent six strand gilt collar by the Japanese artist Yasuki Hiramatsu and a pair of elegant oxidised silver earrings by the Norwegian Tone Vigeland. A brooch by Catalan artist Ramon Puig Cuyàs is one of the few pieces in the collection made from non-precious materials.

As there is still relatively little serious documentation of studio jewellery, Smith collects without reference to catalogues, relying on her own eye and judgement. However, she does own most of the small body of critical literature on the subject, and also keeps accurate records of all her purchases — both signs of the collector rather than a casual buyer. Her observation that she has never regretted a single purchase is testament both to her initial judgement, and to the quality of work which she has bought.

Her purchases are mostly made from private galleries in Britain, which allows her to view and discuss a range of work in some detail. Whether or not she is buying, an important part of developing her interest is to visit as many exhibitions of studio jewellery as possible. Collecting may have its rewards, but it requires a certain amount of dedicated footwork! What is perhaps most astonishing, given the scope of the collection, is that it has not been acquired on a millionaire's bank balance. Careful selection, made patiently over a period of time, has produced a significant collection on the salary of a professional academic.

The knowledge and enthusiasm that Smith and her fellow collectors bring to studio jewellery can stimulate the quality and range of work produced and support artists in the most positive way possible: by allowing them to make a living at what they do. The advantage the private collector has over the public collection, is in the way in which they can show jewellery in its proper context, being worn. The appreciative private collector is one of studio jewellery's most important patrons and one of its best publicists.

The private gallery

If studio jewellers are to sell their work, and collectors and casual buyers are to purchase it, there must be sales outlets. The range and style of these outlets have an undeniable influence on what is produced and bought. The final decades of the twentieth century have seen a significant expansion in the number of sources for purchasing studio jewellery, encompassing private galleries, specialist fairs, group selling exhibitions in temporary venues and shops in public institutions.

Of all these outlets, the private gallery is potentially the most influential. An individual piece of jewellery, like any other work of art, benefits from an environment which allows space for consideration of its individual qualities. Work produced with time and attention to detail, deserves no less time and attention in its presentation and sale. It is reasonable to assume that those who provide the link between maker and buyer will have done their research and understand something about their stock. The staff of private galleries expect to devote a significant amount of their time to discussing the works on display on a one-to-one basis with a client, and will see an emphasis on this individual relationship as vital to the success of the business.

They will regard the building of a similar relationship with the individual artist as equally vital. A good understanding between the two encourages the gallery to take risks with new work and encourages the maker to realise new ideas in the knowledge that the gallery will dedicate time and resources to developing appreciation of the work. Although a good artist/gallery relationship can never guarantee the success of certain types of work, examination of the lives of successful artists usually shows such a relationship to have been important.

Private galleries have been influential in increasing access to contemporary jewellery and promoting an understanding of it, and in this respect a good commercial gallery can have the prestige and influence of a public collection. The history of studio jewellery would be very different, and less interesting, without the efforts of pioneering jewellery galleries such as Electrum in London, Oxford Gallery in Oxford and Galerie Ra in Amsterdam.

To be successful, the private gallery needs to balance education, promotion, business acumen and a concern for accessibility. In such a gallery the visitor will be encouraged to view, handle, try on and discuss a wide range of pieces of jewellery. Such activity is vital to understanding imaginative work, but is virtually impossible in the formal environment of a public gallery, where additionally there may be nobody on hand to answer questions. Such active appreciation may also be difficult in the public hubbub of a busy fair.

Documentary material associated with exhibitions in private galleries can help confer status on different works of art. The increase in well-illustrated catalogues from private galleries is partly due to developments in print technology, which have increased the quality and reduced the costs of production. The increase has also been influenced by an awareness of how good-quality information can create and sustain markets. The scholarly monograph, as much as the price ticket, can act as a commercial tool and an effective dealer bridges the worlds of scholarship and commerce.

The valuing of the individual, essential to studio jewellery, is also essential to the success of the private gallery, which makes it an important environment for looking at studio jewellery. The combined forces of talented maker and informed promoter can begin to have significant impact on the market for individual work.

Social conventions and gender

Of the studio jewellers in this publication over two thirds are women. This female bias may not be surprising in societies in which women tend to be the ones who wear jewellery. However, questions of gender may affect how we view all kinds of jewellery including studio jewellery. The gender issue can be fundamental to understanding the relative value placed on studio jewellery in different societies.

There are a number of ways in which gender influences perception of jewellery today. The most significant is that most men do not wear jewellery; most women do. Since most men do not acquire jewellery to wear themselves, they are often separated from a genuine understanding of its immense potential, and are prevented from developing an interest in it — apart from a financial one. In societies in which the majority of opinion-formers have been male, this will create a barrier to jewellery receiving serious, critical attention. Jewellery is implicitly labelled as a subject of female interest only, and as such is less likely to enter the artistic canon. This bias is clearly illustrated in general books on the history of art and design (written by both men and women), most of which contain no reference to jewellery at all.

The tradition remains, in many societies, that jewellery worn by women is bought by men. This convention of affluent males providing jewellery for dependent females can reinforce gender stereotypes, making jewellery seem an unlikely medium through which to challenge the status quo. But this is far from being the case. In recent decades, there has been a growing interest in new and different forms of jewellery, both from makers and from potential wearers.

Throughout the post-war years, changes in conventions of dress and lifestyle have paved the way for new and different expectations about jewellery generally. As much as we have all benefited from labour-saving devices in the home, so we have been freed from rigidly proscribed conventions about what we can both wear and do. For women, this has meant greater opportunities in the workplace and, by extension, greater economic independence.

The spending power of women has, of course, particular relevance to the field of jewellery. Most women, with centuries of unbroken jewellery wearing behind them, still consider some form of jewellery an important part of their lives, and most own and wear it. Yet what women choose to buy and wear themselves may be very different from work that has been bought for them. As we have seen, jewellery can be used as a powerful means of self-expression.

Although the idea of the serious as

non-adorned, the masculine as anti-decorative, still persists in many societies, men have continued to wear jewellery. In fact, even a cursory glance at the history of male adornment shows the peacock male has never been entirely out of fashion. In recent years, most male jewellery has been confined to the cufflink, tiepin, kiltpin and wristwatch. Interestingly, these are all defined by a practical function, which somehow makes them more acceptably male, however intricate and decorative the individual pieces. Although all these items are jewellery, many of their male wearers would not describe them as such. Men's jewellery can be a covert business.

Men are, however, emerging from the straitjacket convention of suit and no jewels. To some extent, the path to greater decorative freedom has been beaten by the gay community. As part of a bid to challenge orthodoxies about socially acceptable behaviour, gay men have explored different styles of dress and body adornment. This social group has tended to celebrate the theatrical, sexually attractive male who takes pleasure in personal adornment.

Youth culture has been an equally powerful force for change. The young are far less constrained by conventions of dress: on the contrary they have a need to challenge conventions and invent their own. Street fashions, based on continually evolving and often ephemeral conventions, have resulted in exuberant displays of body ornament, including the challenging (although not original) interest in tattooing and body

piercing. Styles like these filter through, in dilute form, to affect the attitudes of wider society. As a result, younger men are almost as likely to be sporting rings, earrings, brooches and necklaces as their female counterparts.

Once the idea of jewellery as something exciting and pleasurable for both men and women has been accepted, it is then a short step to begin discriminating about what kind of jewellery to wear. It soon becomes apparent that if jewellery can enhance a wearer, then jewellery of real, imaginative quality can be a particular enhancement.

Studio jewellers wishing to create work of interest and relevance to society as a whole must address questions of gender, and many do. It is no coincidence that the brooch, in many ways the most unisex form of jewellery, is one of the most common forms used by studio jewellers. Studio jewellers have always been sensitive monitors of change in the art of the wearable, and they are increasingly becoming perceptive commentators on important modern issues concerning personal and cultural identity. Although changing social conventions can be shown to influence studio jewellery, like all forms of art, studio jewellery can also be a powerful agent for change.

THE MAKER'S MARK

A good piece of jewellery feels innately complete, almost as if its appearance was inevitable from the start. It exudes confidence. This impression of effortlessness and immediacy often disguises exceptional skill and much time and work. Peter Chang's exuberant bangles and brooches epitomise this confidence and apparent effortlessness, but they are the product of painstaking, time-consuming mosaic and inlay techniques. One bangle in the collections of the National Museums of Scotland took nearly forty-four hours to make.

The purpose of this section is to approach studio jewellery by looking at how the finished pieces evolve and at the expertise that lies behind them. It is not a guide to technique. Brief explanations of technical terms can be found in the Glossary. Further detailed information can be found in the comprehensive book by Oppi Untracht listed in Further Reading (1982).

Acquiring practical expertise

For most aspiring studio jewellers, acquiring technical skills is the first step in developing their chosen means of expression. Nearly all the jewellers in this book, regardless of their country of origin, have received formal training in jewellery techniques.

Joaquim Capdevila and Mark Powell are two of the surprisingly small number of the jewellers featured here who come from families boasting generations of jewellers, for whom access to tools and techniques was part of daily life. Very few schools in any country provide jewellery training in any depth for a young age group, and most of the jewellers were introduced to basic techniques at art or technical colleges.

Where and how jewellers train can have a fundamental effect on the range and extent of their technical skills, as well as their development of ideas. Access to technical training varies enormously from country to country. In Germany, for instance, all jewellers must undergo a lengthy period of training combining apprenticeship and attendance at a technical college before they are permitted to establish themselves as jewellers.

Nearly all the jewellers in this book studied at art or technical colleges at some point, and many of them have

Grainne Morton in her Edinburgh workshop

pursued further studies at postgraduate level, often abroad, to widen or deepen their experience. It is common for newly-qualified jewellers to work for a period with an experienced maker. For example, the German Rudolph Bott worked with Giampaolo Babetto in Italy. Some attach themselves to specialist craftspeople to develop particular skills.

When jewellers trained is also important. In Britain, for instance, Gerda Flöckinger established an experimental course in jewellery at Hornsey College of Art in 1962 which marked an educational watershed for the subject. It championed a pioneering approach concentrating on the interplay and interdependence of idea and technique. This marked the way forward for studio jewellery in the following decades, and most of the jewellers in this book trained after the establishment of this new direction. Unfortunately, the ensuing years have seen an ever-widening gap between the kind of training offered at art and technical colleges and that provided by the apprenticeship schemes favoured by commercial firms, which are based on supreme craftsmanship but do not encourage innovative design or new approaches to technique.

Technique

Technique is the tool by which ideas are realised, and an understanding of techniques, the practical skills and methods used in making jewellery, is essential for both creation and decoration. The huge range of materials available to studio jewellers requires an even wider grasp of technique if their full potential is to be exploited.

There are numerous ways of constructing a piece of jewellery, but all involve either the shaping of materials or the assembly of separate parts. Carving, which extracts form by cutting from a solid piece of material, can be applied to many different media. Liv Blåvarp, for example, carves wood, Pavel Opočenský carves stone, whilst Dawn Emms applies the same technique to cellulose acetate. Fabrication, the joining of separate parts to form a whole, has been used in the construction of much of the jewellery illustrated in this book, including the work by Sandra Enterline and Gordon Lawrie.

Casting utilises the property of certain materials to liquify when heated, enabling them to be shaped in a mould and allowed to harden, taking on permanent shape. This offers endless possibilities for forming, and has been much exploited by studio jewellers such as Karl Fritsch and Gerd Rothmann. Potentially even more interesting, but less used at present, is electroforming, which can create a permanent metallic form from almost any object of any shape or material (such as a twig, or stiffened paper). Invented in the mid-nineteenth century, its potential for studio jewellery has yet to be extensively explored, but James Bennett, for example, is a noted practitioner.

A large range of decorative techniques is available to studio jewellers. Depending on the material used, these can alter colour (anodising, patination) or texture (engraving, granulation, repoussé and chasing, reticulation), or provide other kinds of surface interest (etching, enamelling, laminating, photoetching, laser-cutting). A few of the many examples featured in this book include anodising aluminium (Jane Adam), engraving (Malcolm Appleby), and enamelling (James Bennett).

Certain techniques have particular cultural resonances, such as the use of *keumboo* by Jung Hoo Kim in Korea, and lacquer and *makie* by Shinya Yamamura in Japan. Interestingly, some culture-specific techniques are being explored far beyond the boundaries of their countries of origin. For example, the lamination technique of *mokume gane*, originally Japanese, is being imaginatively used in Italy by Stefano Marchetti. Some techniques have crossed into jewellery from other disciplines. The adaptation of textile techniques for jewellery, for instance, has provided a particularly rich area for experimentation in recent years. Arline Fisch, one of the earliest exponents of this, has explored all kinds of techniques including weaving, hand and machine knitting and crochet.

Process

Process takes the jeweller from the original idea to the finished object. David Watkins has described how, for jewellers who carry out the whole physical making of jewellery from conception to completion, one of the attractions is that intuition and the senses are actively combined throughout the task (see Further Reading). Studio jewellers constantly explore ideas, develop their understanding of materials and learn from past successes and, sometimes more importantly, their mistakes. Each piece of work can trigger a new idea or suggest a new form. Process is rounded and interconnected, not linear.

How does a jeweller turn the germ of an idea into a finished work? Each individual has their own way of working. Some makers draw on paper first, not necessarily to produce a plan of how a jewel will be made and assembled, but to explore an idea in a quick and simple way. Gerda Flöckinger works surrounded by hundreds of drawings, executed rapidly and fluently, but the creation of the work itself is more improvised, beginning with a basic idea then following a complex route until the piece 'feels right'. She describes it as like composing and performing simultaneously. A few (such as Ann Marie Shillito and David Watkins) have experimented with CAD/CAM which offers its own new perspective.

Other jewellers do not use two-dimensional methods to visualise a three-dimensional object but prefer, like Elizabeth Callinicos and Peter Dvorak, to make three-dimensional models. These may be of the finished piece, or parts of it, and are used to resolve aesthetic questions such as the visual balance and integrity of a work, and practical ones such as the ultimate assembly and how a piece of jewellery may be worn. Models can be made in cheap materials like card, which can be worked quickly, for the maker's time costs money. The making of the models may well alter the final outcome.

Most studio jewellers work directly with their chosen materials, evolving the jewel by drawing on their instincts and experience, working on a piece until it seems complete. They think with their hands and eyes, although they are subconsciously drawing on years of accumulated information. Catherine Truman describes how she carves and carves until the surface is believable. Then she stops. To these jewellers, process is based firmly on the inherent qualities and characteristics of the materials themselves.

Onno Boekhoudt is a dedicated exponent of the use of process itself as a formative method for jewellery. The development of the eventual form of a piece, using simple techniques such as hammering or raising, is completely dependent on the action of producing that piece. He will often create a series of works to explore a concept. Jacqueline Mina uses a completely intuitive process based on her intimate knowledge of gold and how it responds, developed over years of experience. Tone Vigeland starts with the human body. The way her jewellery moves with and hangs on the body provides the key to the sensuality in her work. Grainne Morton starts with the tiny objects she collects and makes.

Jewellers' working environments can also affect process and the outcome of their work. Many studio jewellers assemble objects or illustrations around their workbenches to act as visual prompts. They may surround themselves with inspirational images or objects, perhaps postcards of artworks, or natural objects such as twigs or shells,

none of which will be copied but whose essence will be incorporated into the spirit of their work. The other senses are involved too: many jewellers mention the importance of music to their work.

A dynamic discipline

For a surprising number of people, the path to jewellery has not been direct. Many jewellers in this book originally trained for quite another discipline. Toril Bjorg and Peter Chang, amongst others, studied sculpture, Gerda Flöckinger fine art and etching, Catherine Martin opera singing and textiles, Wendy Ramshaw, Beppe Kessler and Verena Sieber-Fuchs textiles, and Hans Stofer precision engineering, whilst Peter Hoogeboom and Catherine Truman trained as teachers. Kevin Coates still follows parallel careers in music and jewellery. Robert Smit has taken one of the most varied routes. Trained initially as a precision instrument maker, he then studied as a jeweller and was a successful and inventive studio jeweller for many years. He then took a fifteen-year break to concentrate on drawing and painting before returning to jewellery. Artists like Smit can move in and out of the discipline and grow in strength as a result, whilst jewellery itself has benefited from such wide-ranging experiences and backgrounds.

The ability of jewellers to move between relatively small scale work and work on a much larger scale is particularly fascinating. Several of the artists in this book, including Gilles Jonemann, Fritz Maierhofer, Pavel Opočenský and David Watkins, are also

GLOSSARY

sculptors whilst others, such as Susan Cross and Wendy Ramshaw, have produced architectural elements like gates. This flexibility of approach continually refreshes the subject and brings it new experiences, influences and insights. Studio jewellery is a dynamic discipline with multiskilled practitioners.

acid etching
decorative technique involving deliberate removal of areas of metal using chemicals

alloy
a combination of two or more metals

anodising
electrochemical method of forming a coating on metal, often used to provide a surface on aluminium that can be dyed

CAD/CAM
computer-aided design

casting
forming metal in moulds by melting then cooling (various methods)

cellulose acetate
a thermoplastic plastic (can be softened by heating and hardened by cooling without chemical changes taking place)

chasing
making hollows or grooves in metals from the front, using hammer and chasing tools

Colorcore
trademark name of a synthetic laminate made by Formica Corporation

drawing
hand-making wire by pulling metal

through a drawplate with a series of holes of diminishing size

electroforming
method of creating form and surface by the electrodeposition of metal onto another material appropriately prepared via an electrolytic solution

enamel
glass fused on to metal by heat

engraving
cutting incisions into a metal or other material, removing some of the material from the surface in the process

etching
see acid etching

fabrication
the joining of separate parts to form a whole

forging
shaping metal, hot or cold, by hammering

fusing
forming method involving heating metal surfaces to melting point to make fused forms or join parts by atomic interpenetration

fusion inlay
inlay permanently fused to a metal base by heat

granulation
decorative technique involving fusing small metallic balls or granules to a metallic surface, usually in gold, more rarely silver

keumboo
24 ct gold foil overlaid on silver using heat (Korean)

kumihimo
a braiding technique (Japanese)

lacquer
a natural resin from the sap of the sumac tree, built up in layers on a solid base, especially wood

lamination
the bonding together of two or more layers of different metals to produce a composite whole

makie
metal powder (Japanese)

milling
removing metal from a surface by grinding with a rotating cutting tool

mokume gane
literally 'wood-grain metal'; a lamination process involving the fusion of different metal layers, one of which is copper (Japanese)

niello
an alloy of silver, copper and lead melted with sulphur, producing a black metallic sulphide compound used for inlay

oxidising
deliberate tarnishing or colouring of metal using chemicals

patination
deliberate alteration of the natural surface colour of a metal

photoetching
decorative technique for reproducing photographic images on metal

raden
mother-of-pearl (Japanese)

raising
creating shape from sheet metal using hammers

refractory metals
group of metals, including titanium, tantalum and niobium, usually used for their capacity to develop brightly-coloured surface films, but which must be cold-worked or joined due to their extremely high melting points

repoussé
a decorative technique of working metal from the back using a hammer and punches

reticulation
the controlled melting of metallic surfaces to produce texture

samorodok
see reticulation; literally 'born by itself' (Russian)

tantalum
see refractory metals

BIOGRAPHIES

AUSTRALIA

ROBERT BAINES (p21) Born 1949, Australia. Studied RMIT*, Melbourne. Major Collections include: Victoria & Albert Museum, London; National Gallery of Australia, Canberra; National Gallery of Victoria; Galerie am Graben, Austria; Waikato Museum of Art & History, New Zealand.

HELEN BRITTON (p66) Born 1966, Australia. Studied Edith Cowan University, Perth; Curtin University. Major Collections include: Art Gallery of Western Australia; Powerhouse Museum, Sydney.

PIERRE CAVALAN (p70) Born 1954, France. Studied National School for Jewellery, Paris. Moved to Australia 1980 Major Collections include: Powerhouse Museum, Sydney; National Gallery of Australia, Canberra.

ROWENA GOUGH (p26) Born 1958, Australia. Studied RMIT*, Melbourne; Sydney College of Arts. Major Collections include: National Gallery of Australia, Canberra; Art Gallery of Western Australia; Craft Museum,

Frankfurt; State Museum for Applied Arts, Munich.

FIONA KWONG (p68) Born 1971, Australia. Studied RMIT*, Melbourne.

CARLIER MAKIGAWA (p71) Born 1952, Australia. Studied Curtin University; RMIT*, Melbourne. Major Collections include: National Museum of Contemporary Art, Japan; Cooper-Hewitt Museum, New York; Museum of Decorative Arts, Montreal; National Gallery of Australia, Canberra; Art Galleries of Western and South Australia.

SALLY MARSLAND (p64) Born 1969, Australia. Studied RMIT*, Melbourne. Major Collections include: National Gallery of Victoria; Queensland Art Gallery.

CATHERINE TRUMAN (p17) Born 1957, Australia. Studied South Australia College of Art & Education, School of Design. Major Collections include: National Gallery of Australia, Canberra; Powerhouse Museum, Sydney; Art Gallery of South Australia.

AUSTRIA

PETER DVORAK (p46) Born 1954, Czechoslovakia. Studied School for Jewellery and Metals, Turnov. Moved to Austria 1980.

FRITZ MAIERHOFER (p42) Born 1941. Master Craftsman Diploma from Jeweller Anton Heldwein 1966. Major Collections include: National Museums of Scotland, Edinburgh; Applied Arts Museum, Vienna; Schmuckmuseum, Pforzheim; Worshipful Company of Goldsmiths, London; Art Gallery of Western Australia.

CANADA

ALISON BAILEY SMITH (p13) Born 1967, Scotland. Studied Edinburgh College of Art. Moved to Canada 1997. Major Collections include: Aberdeen Art Gallery; National Museums of Scotland, Edinburgh.

BARBARA STUTMAN (p67) Born 1945, Canada. Studied Saidye Bronfman Center, Montreal; Concordia University, Montreal.

CZECH REPUBLIC

RENE HORA (p17) Born 1960, Czechoslovakia. Studied Secondary Art School, Jablonec; College of Applied Arts, Prague. Major Collections include: National Gallery of Slovakia, Bratislava; Gallery of Moravia, Brno.

*Royal Melbourne Institute of Technology

PAVEL OPOCENSKY (p16) Born 1954, Czechoslovakia. Studied School for Jewellery Design, Jablonec; School for Jewellery and Metals, Turnov. Major Collections include: American Craft Museum, New York; State Museum for Applied Arts, Munich; Museum of Applied Arts, Oslo; Museum of Applied Arts, Prague; Slovenian National Gallery, Bratislava; Cooper-Hewitt Museum, New York.

JIRI SIBOR (p45) Born 1966, Czechoslovakia. Studied High Professional School, Kurim; High Technical School for Metals, Kurim. Major Collections include: Museum of Applied Arts, Brno.

DENMARK

KAREN IHLE/JENS ELIASEN (p43) Karen Ihle. Born 1950, Denmark. Studied Goldschmiedefachschule, Pforzheim; Guldsmedehøjskolen, Copenhagen. Jens Eliasen. Born 1951, Denmark. Studied Guldsmedehøjskolen, Copenhagen.
Major Collections include: Art Museum, Tønder; State Art Collection; Collection of Danish Royal Family.

ANETTE KRAEN (p28) Born 1945, Denmark. Studied Guldsmedehojskolen, Copenhagen. Major Collections include: Museum of Decorative Art, Copenhagen; Röhsska Museum, Gothenburg; Museum of Applied Art, Oslo.

PER SUNTUM (p64) Born 1944, Denmark. Studied Guldsmedehøjskolen, Copenhagen. Major Collections include: Museum of Decorative Art, Copenhagen; Danish Arts Foundation; Rohsska Museum, Gothenburg.

THORKILD THOGERSEN (p43) Born 1964, South Africa. Studied Technicon Natal, Durban; Guldsmedehøjskolen, Copenhagen. Major Collections include: Museum of Decorative Arts, Montreal; Museum of Design, Copenhagen.

ENGLAND

JANE ADAM (p24) Born 1954, England. Studied Manchester Polytechnic; Royal College of Art, London. Major Collections include: Cooper-Hewitt Museum, New York; National Museums of Scotland, Edinburgh; Crafts Council, London; Victoria & Albert Museum, London; Museum of Decorative Arts, Helsinki.

ELIZABETH CALLINICOS (p31) Born 1966, England. Studied West Surrey College of Art; Royal College of Art, London. Collections include: Crafts Council, London.

KEVIN COATES (p59) Born 1950, England. Studied Music, Antonio di Palma, Adelaide. Studied Jewellery at Central School of Art and Royal College of Art, London. Major Collections include: Victoria & Albert Museum, London; Worshipful Company of Goldsmiths, London.

CYNTHIA COUSENS (p36) Born 1956, England. Studied Loughborough College of Art; Royal College of Art, London. Major Collections include: National Museums of Scotland, Edinburgh; Victoria & Albert Museum, London; Crafts Council, London; Worshipful Company of Goldsmiths, London; Musee de l'horlogerie, Geneva.

DAWN EMMS (p51) Born 1966, Wales. Studied Middlesex University, London. Major Collections include: National Museums of Scotland, Edinburgh; Crafts Council, London.

GERDA FLOCKINGER CBE (p35) Born 1927, Austria. Moved to England 1938. Studied St. Martins and Central School of Art, London. Major Collections include: National Museums of Scotland, Edinburgh; Victoria & Albert Museum, London; Worshipful Company of Goldsmiths, London; Schmuckmuseum, Pforzheim.

SIMON FRASER (p56) Born 1960, Scotland. Studied Sheffield Polytechnic; Royal College of Art, London. Major Collections include: National Museums of Scotland, Edinburgh; Shipley Art Gallery, Gateshead.

EILEEN GATT (p60) Born 1970, Scotland. Studied Duncan of Jordanstone College of Art, Dundee; Royal College of Art, London.

DAWN GULYAS (p24) Born 1963, England. Studied University of Brighton; Royal College of Art, London. Major Collections include: National Museums of Scotland, Edinburgh; Crafts Council, London.

KATY HACKNEY (p83) Born 1967, Scotland. Studied Edinburgh College of Art; Royal College of Art, London. Major Collections include: National Museums of Scotland, Edinburgh; Crafts Council, London.

MARIA HANSON (p30) Born 1967, England. Studied West Surrey College of Art; Royal College of Art, London. Major Collections include: National Museums of Scotland, Edinburgh; Crafts Council, London.

DAPHNE KRINOS (p79) Born 1955, Greece. Studied Middlesex Polytechnic, London. Major Collections include: Crafts Council, London.

CATHERINE MARTIN (p33) Born 1949, England. Studied Guildhall School of Music, London; Domyo School of Kumihimo, Japan; Royal College of Art, London. Major Collections include: National Museums of Scotland, Edinburgh; Birmingham Museum & Art Gallery; Victoria & Albert Museum, London; Worshipful Company of Goldsmiths, London.

SUSAN MAY (p36) Born 1954, England. Studied Middlesex Polytechnic, London. Major Collections include: Worshipful Company of Goldsmiths, London.

JACQUELINE MINA (p15) Born 1942, England. Studied Hornsey College of Art; Royal College of Art, London. Major Collections include: National Museums of Scotland, Edinburgh; Crafts Council, London; Worshipful Company of Goldsmiths, London; Victoria & Albert Museum, London; Cooper-Hewitt Museum, New York.

WENDY RAMSHAW OBE (p33) Born 1939, England. Studied Newcastle College of Art & Industrial Design; Reading University; Central School of Art & Design. Major Collections include: National Museums of Scotland, Edinburgh; National Gallery of Australia, Canberra; Corning Museum, New York; Crafts Council, London; Museum of Decorative Arts, Paris; Museum of Modern Art, Kyoto; Arts and Crafts Museum, Cologne; Schmuckmuseum, Pforzheim; Stedelijk Museum, Holland; Victoria & Albert Museum, London; Worshipful Company of Goldsmiths, London.

MAH RANA (p73) Born 1964, England. Studied Buckinghamshire College of Art; Royal College of Art, London. Major Collections include: National Museums of Scotland, Edinburgh; Birmingham Museum and Art Gallery; Crafts Council, London.

HANS STOFER (p74) Born 1957, Switzerland. Studied Zurich School of Art. Moved to England 1986. Major Collections include: Crafts Council, London; Cleveland Contemporary Jewellery Collection, Middlesborough.

ESTHER WARD (p43) Born 1964, England. Studied Middlesex Polytechnic and Royal College of Art, London. Major Collections include: Crafts Council, London; Cleveland Contemporary Jewellery Collection, Middlesborough; Cooper-Hewitt Museum, New York.

DAVID WATKINS (p35) Born 1940, England. Studied Reading University. Major Collections include: National Museums of Scotland, Edinburgh; National Gallery of Australia, Canberra; Birmingham Museum and Art Gallery; State Museum for Applied Art, Munich; Museum for Applied Art, Oslo; Arts and Crafts Museum, Hamburg; National Museums of Modern Art, Kyoto & Tokyo; Victoria & Albert Museum, London.

FINLAND

PETTERI IKONEN (p56) Born 1961, Finland. Studied Craft College of Lappeenranta; University of Industrial Arts, Helsinki.

JANNA SYVANOJA (p11) Born 1960, Finland. Studied University of Industrial Arts, Helsinki. Major Collections include: Museum of Applied Arts, Helsinki; Röhsska Museum, Gothenburg; Museum of Decorative Arts, Montreal; National Museum, Stockholm; Museum of Decorative Art, Copenhagen.

FRANCE

MONIKA BRUGGER (p22) Born 1958, Germany. Studied Fachhochschule für Gestaltung, Pforzheim; Academie des Beaux Arts, Antwerp. Major Collections include: Museum of Decorative Arts, Paris.

GILLES JONEMANN (p11) Born 1944 France. Studied Beaux-Arts d'Aix-en-Provence; School of Applied Arts, Paris. Major Collections include: Museum of Decorative Arts, Paris.

GERMANY

ALEXANDRA BAHLMANN (p43) Born 1961, Germany. Studied Rietveld Academy, Amsterdam; Akademie der Bildenden Künste, Munich.

RUDOLF BOTT (p48) Born 1956, Germany. Studied Ziechenakademie, Hanau; Akademie der Bildenden Künste, Munich. Major Collections include: State Museum for Applied Arts, Munich.

BUSSI BUHS (p66) Born 1940, Germany. Studied Academy of Fine Arts, Karlsruhe; Technical College, Karlsruhe.

KARL FRITSCH (p57) Born 1963, Germany. Studied Goldschmeideschule, Pforzheim; Akademie der Bildenden Kunste, Munich.

ELISABETH HOLDER (p62) Born 1950, Germany. Studied Staatliche Zeichenakademie, Hanau; Fachhochschule, Dusseldorf; Royal College of Art, London. Major collections include: National Museums of Scotland, Edinburgh; Arts and Crafts Museum, Berlin; Schmuckmuseum, Pforzheim; National Museum of Modern Art, Kyoto; Victoria & Albert Museum, London.

HILDE JANICH (p76) Born 1953, Germany. Studied Hauptschule, Duisburg; Fachhochschule, Dusseldorf.

IMKE JORNS (p40) Born 1968, Germany. Studied Akademie fur Bildenden Künste, Dresden; Hochschule für Kunst und Design, Halle; Ecole des Beaux Arts, Marseille.

HERMAN JUNGER (p34) Born 1928, Germany. Studied Akademie der Bildenden Künste, Munich. Major Collections include: National Museums of Scotland, Edinburgh; Schmuckmuseum, Pforzheim; Arts and Crafts Museum, Hamburg; Crafts Museum, Frankfurt; Victoria & Albert Museum, London; Art Gallery of Western Australia, Perth.

KATJE KORSAWE (p27) Born 1966, Germany. Studied Technical School, Neu-Gablonz; Fachhochschule, Dusseldorf.

DOROTHEA PRUEHL (p12) Born 1937, Germany. Studied Hochschule für Industrielle Formgestaltung, Halle.

GERD ROTHMANN (p82) Born 1941, Germany. Studied Zeichenakademie, Hanau. Major Collections include: Schmuckmuseum, Pforzheim; Applied Arts Museum, Vienna; National Museum of Modern Art, Tokyo; Stedelijk Museum, Amsterdam; Victoria & Albert Museum, London; Museum of Modern Art, New York.

STEPHAN SEYFFERT (p64) Born 1960. Studied Fachhochschule für Gestaltung, Pforzheim; Akademie der Bildenden Künste, Karlsruhe.

ANETTE WOHLLEBER (p51) Born 1962, Germany. Studied Fachhochschule für Gestaltung, Pforzheim. Nova Scotia College of Art and Design, Halifax. Major Collections include: Schmuckmuseum, Pforzheim.

IRELAND

ALAN ARDIFF (p51) Born 1965, Ireland. Studied National College of Art & Design, Dublin.

BRIGITTE TURBA (p13) Born 1964, Germany. Studied Fachhochschule für Gestaltung, Pforzheim; Kilkenny Workshops, Ireland. Major Collections include: Röhsska Museum, Gothenburg.

ISRAEL

VERED KAMINSKI (p55) Born 1953, Israel. Studied Bezalel Academy, Jerusalem; Rietveld Academy, Amsterdam; Department of Plastic Arts, University of Paris.

ESTHER KNOBEL (p66) Born 1949, Poland. Studied Bezalel Academy, Jerusalem; Royal College of Art, London. Major Collections include: Stedelijk Museum, Amsterdam; Museum of Applied Arts, Vienna; Israel Museum, Jerusalem; Museum of Modern Art, Kyoto; Museum of Decorative Arts, Montreal; Art Gallery of Western Australia; Shipley Art Gallery, Gateshead.

ITALY

GIAMPAOLO BABETTO (p48) Born 1947, Italy. Studied Istituto d'Arte 'P. Selvatico', Padua. Major Collections include: National Museums of Scotland, Edinburgh; Schmuckmuseum, Pforzheim; Victoria & Albert Museum, London; Art Gallery of Western Australia; Museum of Decorative Arts, Paris; Arts and Crafts Museum, Hamburg.

GIOVANNI CORVAJA (p39) Born 1971, Italy. Studied Istituto d'Arte, 'P. Selvatico', Padua; Royal College of Art, London. Major Collections include: Museum of Decorative Arts, Montreal; Museum of Decorative Arts, Paris.

STEFANO MARCHETTI (p39) Born 1970, Italy. Studied Istituto d'Arte, 'P. Selvatico', Padua; Accademia di Belle Arti, Venice.

BARBARA PAGANIN (p63) Born 1961, Italy. Studied Accademia di Belle Arti, Venice. Major Collections include: Museum of Modern Art, Venice; Boymans van Beuningen Museum, Rotterdam; Museum of Decorative Arts, Montreal; Museum of Decorative Arts, Paris.

FRANCESCO PAVAN (p32) Born 1937, Italy. Studied Istituto d'Arte 'P. Selvatico', Padua. Major Collections include: Schmuckmuseum, Pforzheim; Danner Stiftung, Munich.

ANNAMARIA ZANELLA (p22) Born 1966, Italy. Studied Istituto d'Arte, 'P. Selvatico', Padua; Accademia di Belle Arti, Venice. Major Collections include: Museum of Modern Art, Venice; Museum of Decorative Arts, Paris.

JAPAN

SUO EMIKO (p38) Born 1966, Japan. Studied Tokyo National University of Fine Arts and Music. Major Collections include: State Museum for Applied Arts, Munich.

YASUKI HIRAMATSU (p15) Born 1926, Japan. Studied Tokyo National University of Fine Arts and Music. Major Collections include: Schmuckmuseum, Pforzheim; National Museums of Scotland, Edinburgh; Victoria & Albert Museum, London.

KASUKO MITSUSHIMA (p63) Born 1946, Japan. Studied Jewellery Design, Tokyo; Pilchuck Glass School, USA. Major Collections include: Corning Museum of Glass, New York.

SUNAO SERA (p60) Born 1962, Japan. Studied Womens Junior Art College and with Wahei Ikezawa.

SHINYA YAMAMURA (p23) Born 1960, Japan. Studied Kanazawa College of Art. Major Collections include: Victoria & Albert Museum, London.

KOREA

EUN-MEE CHUNG (p53) Born 1959, Korea. Studied Hong-Ik University, Seoul; University of Wisconsin, USA.

JUNG-HOO KIM (p54) Born 1959, Korea. Studied Seoul National University; State University of New York. Major Collections include: Cooper-Hewitt Museum, New York; Corning Museum of Glass, New York; Museum of Fine Arts, Boston; Victoria & Albert Museum, London; Powerhouse Museum, Sydney; Schmuckmuseum, Pforzheim; Museum of Decorative Arts, Montreal.

SEUNG-HEE KIM (p63) Born 1947, Korea. Studied Seoul National University; Indiana University, USA. Major Collections include: National Museum of Contemporary Art, Seoul.

JUNG-GYU YI (p31) Born 1957, Korea. Studied Han Nam University, Korea; Fachhochschule für Gestaltung, Pforzheim; Ecole Nationale Superieure des Arts Appliqués, Paris.

NETHERLANDS

GIJS BAKKER (p25) Born 1942, Netherlands. Studied Rietveld Academy, Amsterdam; Konstfack Skolan, Stockholm. Major Collections include: Stedelijk Museum, Amsterdam; Powerhouse Museum, Sydney; Cooper-Hewitt Museum, New York; Victoria & Albert Museum, London.

LAURA BAKKER (p62) Born 1954, Netherlands. Studied Vakschool Schoonhoven; Rietveld Academy, Amsterdam. Major Collections include: Israel Museum, Jerusalem; National Museums of Scotland, Edinburgh; Museum of Modern Art, Arnhem.

DINIE BESEMS (p57) Born 1966, Netherlands. Studied Rietveld Academy, Amsterdam. Major Collections include: Stedelijk Museum, Amsterdam

ONNO BOEKHOUDT (p57) Born 1944, Netherlands. Studied Vakschool, Schoonhoven; Kunst und Werkschule, Pforzheim. Major Collections include: Powerhouse Museum, Sydney; Central Museum, Utrecht.

JACOMYN VAN DER DONK (p81) Born 1963, Netherlands. Studied Rietveld Academy, Amsterdam. Major Collections include: Stedelijk Museum, Amsterdam; Museum of Modern Art, Arnhem.

PETER HOOGEBOOM (p20) Born 1961, Netherlands. Studied Rietveld Academy, Amsterdam; Fachhochschule für Gestaltung, Pforzheim.

BEPPE KESSLER (p18) Born 1952, Netherlands. Studied Free University, Amsterdam; Rietveld Academy, Amsterdam. Major Collections include: Stedelijk Museum, Amsterdam; Art and Industry Museum, Trondheim; Museum of Decorative Arts, Montreal.

FELIEKE VAN DER LEEST (p68) Born 1968, Netherlands. Studied Vakschool, Schoonhoven; Rietveld Academy, Amsterdam. Major Collections include: Dutch Textile Museum, Tilburg.

NEL LINSSEN (p10) Born 1935, Netherlands. Studied Academy of Fine Arts, Arnhem. Major Collections include: Stedelijk Museum, Amsterdam; National Museums of Scotland, Edinburgh; Arts and Crafts Museum, Hamburg; Musée d'Horlogerie, Geneva; Museum of Decorative Arts, Lausanne; Cooper-Hewitt Museum, New York; Museum of Applied Arts, Oslo; Museum of Decorative Arts, Montreal.

ANNELIES PLANTEYDT (p37) Born 1956 Netherlands. Studied Rietveld Academy, Amsterdam. Major Collections include: Stedelijk Museum, Amsterdam; National Gallery, Bratislava; Boymans van Beuningen Museum, Rotterdam; Museum of Modern Art, Arnhem.

ROBERT SMIT (p16) Born 1941, Netherlands. Studied Technical School Voor Delft En Omstreken; Kunst und Werkschule, Pforzheim. Major Collections include: Stedelijk Museum, Amsterdam; Museum of Modern Art, Arnhem; Schmuckmuseum, Pforzheim.

NEW ZEALAND

WARWICK FREEMAN (p55) Born 1953, New Zealand. Studied with Peter Woods (Australia); Graham Shirley and Jens Hansen. Major Collections include: Auckland Museum; National Gallery of Australia, Canberra; National Gallery, Victoria; Powerhouse Museum, Sydney.

ARETA WILKINSON (p55) Born 1969, New Zealand. Studied Carrington Polytechnic; Auckland University. Major Collections include: Auckland War Memorial Museum.

NORWAY

TORIL BJORG (p14) Born 1944, Norway. Studied National College of Art & Design, Oslo. Major Collections include: Museums of Applied Art, Bergen, Oslo, Trondheim; Röhsska Museum, Gothenburg.

LIV BLAVARP (p26) Born 1956, Norway. Studied National College of Art & Design, Oslo; Royal College of Art, London. Major Collections include: Museums of Applied Art, Bergen, Oslo, Trondheim; Art Museum of North Norway, Tromsø; Museum of Applied Art, Copenhagen; Arts and Crafts Museum, Berlin; National Museum, Stockholm; Röhsska Museum, Gothenburg; Cooper-Hewitt Museum, New York.

LILLAN ELIASSEN (p67) Born 1961, Norway. Studied National College of Art & Design, Oslo. Major Collections include: Museums of Applied Art, Bergen, Oslo, Trondheim; Museum of Applied Art, Copenhagen.

TONE VIGELAND (p80) Born 1938, Norway. Studied National College of Art & Design, Oslo; Oslo Yrkesskole for gullsmeder. Major Collections include: Cooper-Hewitt Museum, New York; Museums of Applied Art, Bergen, Oslo, Trondheim; Museum of Applied Art, Copenhagen; Museum of Decorative Arts, Paris; National Museum, Stockholm; National Museums of Scotland, Edinburgh; Schmuckmuseum, Pforzheim; Museum of Modern Art, New York; National Museum of Modern Art, Tokyo; Victoria & Albert Museum, London.

SCOTLAND

MALCOLM APPLEBY (p63) Born 1946, England. Studied Ravensbourne, Central, Sir John Cass & Royal College of Art, London. Moved to Scotland, 1969. Major Collections include: Victoria & Albert Museum, London; National Museums of Scotland, Edinburgh; Worshipful Company of Goldsmiths, London; Aberdeen Art Gallery; Fitzwilliam Museum, Cambridge.

PETER CHANG (p24) Born 1944, England. Studied Liverpool College of Art; Slade School of Art, London. Moved to Scotland, 1984. Major Collections include: National Museums of Scotland, Edinburgh; Aberdeen Art Gallery; Victoria & Albert Museum, London; Crafts Council, London; Museum of Decorative Arts, Montreal; Museum for Applied Art, Cologne.

GRAHAM CRIMMINS (p39) Born 1946, England. Studied Birmingham College of Art. Moved to Scotland 1973. Major Collections include: National Museums of Scotland, Edinburgh; Röhsska Museum, Gothenburg; American Crafts Council; Aberdeen Art Gallery; Crafts Council, London.

SUSAN CROSS (p78) Born 1964, England. Studied Middlesex Polytechnic, London. Moved to Scotland 1989. Major Collections include: Crafts Council, London; Victoria & Albert Museum, London; Worshipful Company of Goldsmiths.

JACK CUNNINGHAM (p53) Born 1953, Scotland. Studied Duncan of Jordanstone College of Art, Dundee; Jordanhill College of Education. Major Collections include: National Museums of Scotland, Edinburgh; Kelvingrove Art Gallery, Glasgow; Aberdeen Art Gallery.

ANNE FINLAY (p44) Born 1953, Scotland. Studied Grays School of Art, Aberdeen. Major Collections include: National Museums of Scotland, Edinburgh; Aberdeen Art Gallery; Kyoto National Museum, Japan; Arts and Crafts Museum, Hamburg.

ANNA GORDON (p37) Born 1971, Scotland. Studied Edinburgh College of Art. Major Collections include: National Museums of Scotland, Edinburgh.

DOROTHY HOGG (p30) Born 1945, Scotland. Studied Glasgow School of Art; Royal College of Art, London. Major Collections include: National Museums of Scotland; Crafts Council, London; Worshipful Company of Goldsmiths, London.

GRAINNE MORTON (p41) Born 1970, Ireland. Studied Edinburgh College of Art; Kilkenny Workshops. Major Collections include: National Museums of Scotland.

MARK POWELL (p45) Born 1959, England. Studied Duncan of Jordanstone College of Art, Dundee. Major Collections include: National Museums of Scotland, Edinburgh; Aberdeen Art Gallery; Birmingham Museum and Art Gallery.

GEOFF ROBERTS (p72) Born 1953, England. Studied Birmingham College of Art; Royal College of Art, London. Moved to Scotland 1992. Major Collections include: National Museums of Scotland, Edinburgh; Aberdeen Art Gallery; Shipley Art Gallery, Gateshead.

ANN MARIE SHILLITO (p44) Born 1947, England. Studied Birmingham College of Art; Royal College of Art, London. Moved to Scotland 1978. Major Collections include: National Museums of Scotland; Worshipful Company of Goldsmiths, London; Stoke on Trent Art Gallery.

SLOVAK REPUBLIC

ANTON CEPKA (p45) Born 1936, Slovakia. Studied Kunstgewerbeschule, Bratislava; Hochschule für Angewandte Kunst, Prague. Major Collections include: Schmuckmuseum, Pforzheim; Museum for Applied Arts, Vienna; Stedelijk Museum, Amsterdam; National Gallery of Victoria, Melbourne; National Gallery of Slovakia, Bratislava; Museum of Applied Arts, Prague;.

SPAIN

JOAQUIM CAPDEVILA (p70) Born 1944, Spain. Studied Massana School, Barcelona; Atelier Lacambra, Paris. Major Collections include: Schmuckmuseum, Pforzheim; Arts and Crafts Museum, Hamburg.

RAMON PUIG CUYAS (p59) Born 1953, Spain. Studied Massana School, Barcelona. Major Collections include: Schmuckmuseum, Pforzheim; Museum of Applied Art, Copenhagen; Museum of Decorative Arts, Montreal; Cooper-Hewitt Museum, New York; National Museums of Scotland, Edinburgh.

XAVIER DOMENECH (p42) Born 1960, Spain. Studied Massana School, Barcelona. Major Collections include: National Museums of Scotland, Edinburgh; Arts and Crafts Museum, Hamburg.

JUDY McCAIG (p59) Born 1957, Scotland. Studied Dundee College of Art; Royal College of Art; Chelsea & Central Schools of Art, London. Moved to Spain 1990. Major Collections include: Crafts Council, London.

XAVIER INES I MONCLUS (p51) Born 1966, Spain. Studied Massana School, Barcelona.

SWEDEN

CHRISTER JONSSON (p70) Born 1945, Sweden. Studied National University College of Arts, Craft & Design, Stockholm; University of Arts and Crafts, Helsinki. Major Collections include: National Museum, Stockholm; Röhsska Museum, Gothenburg; Museum of Applied Arts, Copenhagen.

SWITZERLAND

ESTHER BRINKMANN (p83) Born 1953, Switzerland. Studied Ecole des Arts Decoratifs, Geneva. Major Collections include: Musée de l'horlogerie, Geneva; Museum of Decorative Arts, Lausanne.

VERENA SIEBER-FUCHS (p13) Born 1943, Switzerland. Studied School of Decorative Arts, Basle; Applied Arts School, Zurich. Major Collections include: Museum of Decorative Arts, Lausanne; Stedelijk Museum, Amsterdam; Museum of Decorative Arts, Paris; Museum of Applied Art, Frankfurt.

CAROLE GUINARD (p39) Born 1955, Argentina. Studied Ecole des Arts Decoratifs, Geneva; School of Museum of Fine Arts, Boston. Major Collections include: Museum of Decorative Arts, Paris; Museum of Decorative Arts, Lausanne.

SOPHIE HANAGARTH (p67) Born 1968, Switzerland. Studied Ecole des Arts Appliqués Superieurs, Geneva.

SONIA MOREL (p76) Born 1968, Switzerland. Studied Ecole des Arts Appliqués Superieurs, Geneva.

USA

JAMES BENNETT (p22) Born 1948, USA. Studied State University of New York; University of Georgia. Major Collections include: American Museum of Art, Washington; Museum of Applied Art, Oslo; American Craft Museum, New York; Victoria & Albert Museum, London.

JOYCE CHATEAUVERT (p18) Born 1960, USA. Studied University of Iowa.

SANDRA ENTERLINE (p47) Born 1960, USA. Studied Rhode Island School of Design; Rochester Institute of Technology. Major Collections include: American Craft Museum, New York; Oakland Museum, California.

ARLINE FISCH (p79) Born 1931, USA. Studied Skidmore College, New York; University of Illinois; Kunsthaandvaerkerskolen, Copenhagen. Major Collections include: American Craft Museum, New York; Art Gallery of Western Australia; Boston Museum of Fine Art; National Museum of Modern Art, Kyoto; Schmuckmuseum, Pforzheim; National Museums of Scotland, Edinburgh; Victoria & Albert Museum, London.

GORDON LAWRIE (p48) Born 1947, England. Studied Sir John Cass School of Art, London; University of Texas, El Paso.

BRUCE METCALF (p54) Born 1949, USA. Studied Syracuse University; Tyler School of Art, Philadelphia. Major Collections include: American Craft Museum, New York; Museum of Decorative Arts, Montreal.

JOAN PARCHER (p19) Born 1956, USA. Studied Rhode Island School of Design. Major Collections include: American Craft Museum, New York; Renwick Gallery, Smithsonian Institution, Washington; Cooper-Hewitt Museum, New York.

MARJORIE SCHICK (p23) Born 1941, USA. Studied University of Wisconsin; Indiana University; Sir John Cass School of Art, London. Major Collections include: American Craft Museum, New York; Museum of Applied Art, Oslo; National Museum of Modern Art, Kyoto; Victoria & Albert Museum, London.

JOYCE SCOTT (p66) Born 1948, USA. Studied Maryland Institute, Baltimore; Instituto Allende, Mexico; Haystack Mountain School of Crafts, Maine. Major Collections include: Baltimore Museum of Art; Kruithuis Museum, Netherlands; Detroit Institute of Arts.

LISA SPIROS (p47) Born 1959, USA. Studied State University of New Paltz; Munich Academy of Fine Arts, Germany.

RACHELLE THIEWES (p77) Born 1952, USA. Studied Western Illinois University; Kent State University. Major Collections include: American Craft Museum, New York; Art Institute of Chicago; Renwick Gallery, Smithsonian Institution, Washington.

KIWON WANG (p28) Born 1962, USA. Studied Georgia State University; Rhode Island School of Design.

WALES

GAVIN FRASER-WILLIAMS (p48) Born 1966, Wales. Studied Brighton Polytechnic; Royal College of Art, London.

AFTERWORD

Jewellery Moves has suggested ways of seeing and enjoying contemporary studio jewellery. Within the limited space of one publication, the authors have attempted to illustrate the richness, and diversity, of the field, and to celebrate the achievements of 129 artists from 24 different countries. Inevitably, we can only show the tip of the iceberg. If, however, we have managed to communicate at least some of the skill, passion and vision of these artists, then we have succeeded with our principal aims.

For those of you sufficiently inspired by some of the images you have seen, we would encourage you to seek out more examples of studio jewellery by visiting galleries, museums and specialist fairs in your own area. We guarantee you years of pleasure to come.

FURTHER READING

Anderson, P *Contemporary Jewellery in Australia and New Zealand* G & B Arts International, 1998

Cartlidge, B *Twentieth-Century Jewelry* H N Abrams Inc, New York, 1985

Derrez, P *Passion and Profession — Jewellery in past, present and future* Galerie Ra, Amsterdam, 1996

Dormer, P & Turner, R *The New Jewelry — Trends and Traditions* London, Thames & Hudson 1984, 1994

Drutt English, H W & P Dormer *Jewelry of Our Time — Art, Ornament and Obsession* Thames and Hudson, Singapore, 1995

Fisher, A *Africa Adorned* Collins, London, 1984

Jang Sin Goo *Zeitgenossische Schmuckkunst in Korea/Contemporary Korean Jewellery* Schmuckmuseum Pforzheim, 1994

Lewin, S G *American Art Jewelry Today* Thames and Hudson, London, 1994

Lohmann, J *Nordic Jewellery* Nyt Nordisk Forlag Arnold & Funder, L Busck, Copenhagen, 1995

Margetts, M (ed) *International Crafts* Thames and Hudson, Singapore, 1991

Musée des Arts Décoratifs *IIIème Triennale Du Bijou* Editions du May, Paris, 1992

National Museum of Modern Art, Tokyo *Contemporary Jewellery* Tokyo, 1995

Orfebres, F A D *La joia de la joia catalana actual* Electa, Madrid, 1993

Nickl, P (ed) *Schmuck '96/Schmuck '97* Munich 1996/7

Nickl, P (ed) *Talente '96/Talente '97* Munich 1996/7

Phillips, C *Jewelry: From Antiquity to the Present* Thames & Hudson, London, 1996

Poston, D *What is Jewellery?* Crafts Council, London, 1995

Turner, R *Jewelry in Europe and America, New Times, New Thinking* Thames and Hudson, London, 1996

Untracht, O *Jewelry Concepts and Technology* Hale, London, 1982

Untracht, O *Traditional Jewelry of India* Thames & Hudson, London, 1997

Watkins, D *The Best in Contemporary Jewellery* Quarto plc, Switzerland, 1993

GALLERIES

All the galleries listed have active programmes for contemporary jewellery or are specialist jewellery galleries. This is not an exhaustive list of galleries, internationally, but many of the artists illustrated in *Jewellery Moves* will exhibit at the listed galleries.

AUSTRALIA
Gallery Funaki, 4 Crossley Street, Melbourne, Australia 3000

AUSTRIA
Galerie V & V, Bauernmarkt 19, A 1010 Vienna

CANADA
Galerie Noel Guyomarc'h, 460 Ste-Catherine Ouest, Suite 314, Montreal, Quebec H3B 1A7

Harbinger Gallery, 22 Dupont Street East, Waterloo, Ontario, N2J 2G9

DENMARK
Galerie Metal, Nubrodgade 26, Copenhagen K, DK 1203

ENGLAND
Contemporary Applied Arts, 2 Percy Street, London W1

Crafts Council Shop at V&A, Victoria & Albert Museum, South Kensington, London SW7 2RL

Electrum, 21 South Molton Street, London W1Y 1DD

Lesley Craze Gallery, 34 Clerkenwell Green, London EC1R ODU

Oxford Gallery, 23 High Street, Oxford OX1 4AH

FINLAND
Lapponia Jewelry OY, PO Box 72, SF 00511 Helsinki

FRANCE
Galerie Hélène Porée, 31 rue Daguerre, 75014 Paris

GERMANY
Galerie Biró, Zieblandstrasse 19, 80799 Munich

Galerie Cebra, Franklinstrasse 46, D 4000, Dusseldorf 30

Galerie Spektrum, Turkenstrasse 37, D 80799, Munich

IRELAND
Design Yard, 12 East Essex Street, Dublin 2

ITALY
Studio GR 20, Via dei Soncin 27, Padua

JAPAN
Miharudo Gallery, 3-14-18 Meijiro, Toshima-ku, Tokyo 171

KOREA
Craft House, Seoul

NETHERLANDS
Galerie Marzee, Ganzenheuvel 33, NL 6511 WD Nijmegen

Galerie Ra, Vijzelstraat 80, NL 1017, HL Amsterdam

Galerie Louise Smit, Prinsengracht 615, NL 1016 HT Amsterdam

NEW ZEALAND
Crafts Council Gallery, 22 The Terrace, Wellington

NORWAY
Kunsthåndverkerne Kongensgate, Radhusgt. 24, N 0158, Oslo 1

SCOTLAND
The Scottish Gallery, 16 Dundas Street, Edinburgh EH 3 6HZ

Roger Billcliffe Fine Art, 134 Blythswood Street, Glasgow G2 4EL

SPAIN
Hipotesi, rambla de Catalunya 105, SP 08008, Barcelona

JEWELLERS GROUPS, ARTS/CRAFTS COUNCILS

SWITZERLAND

Schmuckforum, Zolikerstrasse 6, CH 8001 Zurich

Galerie a, 34 rue de la filature, 1227 Carouge

USA

Susan Cummins Gallery, 12 Miller Avenue, Mill Valley CA 94941

Helen Drutt Gallery, 1721 Walnut Street, Philadelphia, PA 19103

Jewelers Werk, 2000 Pennsylvania Avenue NW, Washington DC 20006

Joanne Rapp Gallery/The Hand and the Spirit, 4222 North Scottsdale Road, Scottsdale, Arizona 85251

All these organisations may have further information on training, exhibitions and events in their areas.

AUSTRALIA

Crafts Council of Australia, 35 George Street, The Rocks, Sydney NSW 2000

CANADA

Canadian Crafts Council, 189 Laurier Avenue East, Ottawa ON K1N 6P1

DENMARK

Danish Silversmiths, Guldsmedehøjskolen, Vaerkstedvej 5, DK 2500 Valby

ENGLAND

Association of British Jewellery Designers, School of Jewellery, Birmingham Institute of Art and Design, Vittoria Street, Birmingham

Crafts Council, 44A Pentonville Road, London N1 9HF

Worshipful Company of Goldsmiths, Foster Lane, London EC2V 6BN

FINLAND

Artisaani, Unioninkatu 28, SF 00100 Helsinki

GERMANY

Forum für Schmuck und Design E.V. Lutticherstrasse 47, D 5000 Cologne 1

IRELAND

Crafts Council of Ireland, Powerscourt Townhouse Centre, South William Street, Dublin 2

JAPAN

Nitten, 3-8-5 Sendagi Bunkyo-ku, Tokyo 113

NEW ZEALAND

Crafts Council of New Zealand, 22 The Terrace, Wellington, PO Box 498, Wellington 1NZ

SCOTLAND

Scottish Arts Council, 12 Manor Place, Edinburgh EH3 7DD

SWEDEN

Foreningen fur Nutida Svenskt Silver, PO Box 5229, S 102 45 Stockholm

USA

American Crafts Council, 72 Spring Street, New York NY 10012

Society of North American Goldsmiths, 5009 Londonderry Drive, Tampa, FL 33647

WALES

Welsh Arts Council, Holst House, 9 Museum Place, Cardiff CF1 3NX

ACKNOWLEDGEMENTS

Dorothy Hogg, Head of Jewellery, Edinburgh College of Art

Miharu Ando, Miharudo Gallery; Onno Boekhoudt; Aggie Beynon; Julie Blyfield; Barbara Cartlidge, Electrum Gallery; Jack Cunningham; Paul Derrez, Galerie Ra; Mari Funaki, Gallery Funaki; Irena Goldscheider; Graziella Grassetto, GR 20; Noel Guyomarc'h, Galerie Noel Guyomarc'h; Elisabeth Holder; Hungarian/Polish Cultural Institutes; Myung-ok Jeon; Charon Kransen; Gina Matchitt; Marianne Schwlinksi, Galerie Spektrum; Alison Bailey Smith; Hans Stofer; Susan Wraight

Simon Donald; Lesley-Ann Liddiard; Fiona Salvesen

Photography:
Black & white portrait photographs by Carol Gordon (except Simon Fraser, Street Scene by Patrick Denis; workshop photography by Neil McLean).
Carol Gordon graduated from Napier University with a BA (Distinction) in Photography 1991. She lives and works in Edinburgh.

Other Photo Credits: Neil McLean (NMS); A Anders (Bahlmann, Germany); Terje Agnalt (Bjorg, Norway); Ian Atkinson (Cross, Scotland); Rien Bazen (Bakker, G, Netherlands); Jean Beining (Planteydt, Netherlands); Peter Bliek (Linssen, Netherlands); H Schlutze-Brinkop (Pruehl, Germany); Bob Cramp (Ramshaw, England); David Cripps (Watkins, England); Joel Degen (Hackney, Mina, England); Jochen Grun (Bott, Germany); Jewelry Photo Co (Sera, Japan); Eva Jünger (Jünger, Germany); G Pollmiller (Schick, USA); Antonia Reeve (Powell, Scotland); Miroslav Zavadil (Sibor, Czech Republic).

We would like to thank The Society of Jewellery Historians, Department of Scientific Research, The British Museum, London WC1B 3DG, for their contribution to the cost of producing this book.

Particular thanks to Christina Jansen and the Directors, The Scottish Gallery, 16 Dundas Street, Edinburgh EH3 6HZ, 0131 558 1200 and to all friends, collectors, individual models and fellow enthusiasts for their support and encouragement. And, of course, to all artists included in this publication.